Hans-J. Ullmann
Evamaria Ull

Poodles

Standard, Miniature, and Toy Poodles

Everything about Purchase, Training,
Nutrition, and Diseases

With Color Photographs by Outstanding Animal Photographers
and Drawings by Sepp Arnemann

Barron's

Front cover: Miniature Poodles, apricot and white, with Puppy Clips.
Inside front cover: Miniature Poodle, apricot.
Inside back cover: Three Miniature Poodles—silver, apricot, and white—from the Schongau Kennel.
Back cover: (above) Miniature Poodles, apricot and silver.
Back cover: (below) Miniature Poodles, white, black; Standard Poodle, brown.

First English language edition published in 1984 by Barron's Educational Series, Inc.
© 1982 by Gräfe and Unzer GmbH, Munich, West Germany.

The title of the German edition is *Pudels*.

Translated by Rita and Robert Kimber

All inquiries should be addressed to:
Barron's Educational Series, Inc.
250 Wireless Boulevard
Hauppauge, New York 11788

International Standard Book No. 0-8120-2812-0

PRINTED IN HONG KONG
456   490   17 16 15 14 13

Cover Design

Constanze Reithmayr-Frank

Photographs

Animal/Thompson: p. 64 above right and left
Bartl: back cover (above right), p. 10 (below right)
Hinz: front cover; p. 10 (above left and right), pp. 28, 64 (below right)
Institute for Study of Domestic Animals, University of Kiel: p. 46 (above left and right)
Reinhard: inside front cover
Röhl-Herrlich: back cover (below left), p. 27 (above left), p. 45 (above right)
Ullmann: inside back cover, back cover (above left, below right), pp. 9, 10 (below left), p. 27 (above right, below), p. 45 (above left, below), p. 46 (below left and right), pp. 63, 64 (below left)

Important Notes
This pet owner's manual tells the reader how to buy and care for a poodle. The author and the publisher consider it important to point out that the advice given in the book is meant primarily for normally developed puppies from a reputable pet store or a good breeder — that is, dogs of excellent physical health and flawless character.

Anyone who takes on a fully grown dog should be aware that the animal has already formed its basic impressions of human beings. The new owner should watch the animal carefully — especially its behavior toward humans — and meet the previous owner. If the dog comes from a shelter, it may be possible to get some information on the dog's background and peculiarities there. As a result of bad experiences with humans, certain dogs may behave in an unnatural manner or even bite. Only people who have had considerable experience with dogs should consider taking in such an animal.

Even well-behaved and carefully supervised dogs sometimes do damage to someone else's property or cause accidents. It is therefore in the owner's interest to be adequately insured against such eventualities, and we strongly urge all dog owners to purchase a liability policy that covers their dog.

Contents

Contents

Preface

The painter Albrecht Dürer, the philosopher Arthur Schopenhauer, and the poets Eduard Mörike, Heinrich Heine, and—last but not least—Johann Wolfgang von Goethe all succumbed to the charm of poodles and have immortalized the breed in their work. You are therefore in good company if you are interested in poodles. Among the many breeds of dogs that exist, poodles have gained fame for possessing all the qualities that humans value most in dogs. Their amazing intelligence and eagerness to learn, their "classical" beauty, and their unerring sense of loyalty have always been appreciated and admired.

Whether you already own a poodle or are just contemplating buying one, you should learn all you can about every aspect of this interesting creature to make sure your experience with it will be a happy one. In owning a dog, as in any other enterprise, "know-how" is an important prerequisite for success. This pet owner's guide offers you knowledge and the most up-to-date insights from behavioral scientists, veterinarians, and breeders on the topics of buying, raising, feeding, caring for, and training poodles.

We also discuss possible dangers, diseases, and behavioral problems and how they can be avoided.

We are animal photographers by profession, and in the course of years of work we have met a great many poodles as well as their owners and breeders. But our best "object of study" has been and still is a female Miniature Poodle belonging to the mother of one of us. We became so intrigued with the subject of poodles that studying them and everything connected with them became an avocation. Our pursuit of knowledge was much facilitated by the contacts we had made over the years with poodle experts and breeders.

We are especially grateful to Dr. Peter Hollmann, veterinarian and poodle owner in Beuerberg, and Mrs. Ludowicka Bertelmann, owner of the Schongau Poodle Kennel in Upper Bavaria. We have incorported into this guide many useful tips and valuable lessons derived from their years of experience. Some of the pictures in this book were taken at Mrs. Bertelmann's kennels, which have consistently produced prize-winning poodles for years. We would also like to thank Mr. Sepp Arnemann, who, in his drawings, has succeeded in capturing the special poodle quality very well.

This pet owner's guide also discusses the topic "Dogs and Children." Young poodle enthusiasts, who will also be members of your poodle's "pack" day in and day out, have to learn how to treat their pet properly. It is up to parents to teach their children that loving an animal means not just petting it and playing with it but also includes doing some chores and taking responsibility for it. We have written this guide in such a way that children of school age can read and understand it by themselves.

We wish all our readers, both young and old, success and pleasure in their efforts to establish a happy relationship with their dog.

Evamaria Ullmann
Hans-J. Ullmann

Considerations Before You Buy

Is a Poodle the Right Dog for You?

A poodle enthusiast has an unusually wide array of choices from which to select a pet.

No other breed of dog comes in as many sizes and colors as the poodle, and no other dog surpasses it in intelligence, eagerness to learn, adaptability, or loyalty. The poodle is, in a word, the ideal dog. The question at the head of this section might therefore more properly read "Are you the right person for a poodle?"

You may answer this question with a "yes" if you are a true animal lover—that is, if you intend to keep, train, and look after your dog with its nature and needs in mind. In addition, you must be willing to faithfully care for the animal for as long as it lives, even if it should fall ill.

Poodles ordinarily live ten to twelve years; healthy ones living under optimal conditions may live to be fourteen or fifteen, occasionally even older. You should therefore ask yourself honestly whether you are prepared to look after a dog for so long. It is easy in a burst of enthusiasm to acquire a bouncy little fur ball of a puppy. But once the dog has adjusted to you, your family, and your home, you cannot simply pass it on to someone else because you decide that keeping a dog is too much trouble after all. Anyone who gets rid of a dog without compelling reasons, after it has become used to its home, is surely no animal lover.

You should also think ahead and ask yourself how your poodle will be taken

Every poodle is not like every other poodle. This becomes most obvious when you look at a Standard Poodle standing next to a Toy Poodle.

care of when you have to be away from home or if you want to go on a vacation without it. It is not always possible to take a dog along on a trip, and not everybody has friends or neighbors who are able to look after a pet that has to be left behind.

Another point to consider is that grooming is of particular importance for poodles. The characteristic look of a poodle depends much more than with any other breed on the condition of its coat, and a neglected poodle cuts a sorry figure. In addition to the time and patience required daily for grooming, you will have to spend money for trimming every six to eight weeks, unless you want to take on this rather tedious task yourself. If you do not have much time and are unwilling to spend money for grooming and trimming, you may be better off with a breed that requires less upkeep.

Considerations Before You Buy

Prerequisites for Keeping a Dog

To avoid disappointments on the part of both human and dog, all future poodle owners should be aware of the necessary requirements for keeping a dog. Let us begin with your living quarters.

If you have a large apartment or your own home with a yard, there is no problem. Even a Standard Poodle will be comfortable in your home.

If you live in an apartment of average size, you will do better sharing it with a Miniature Poodle.

A small apartment is suitable only for a Toy Poodle, and you will have to be sure to take your dog out for regular walks. Older people often favor Toy Poodles because they are easy to handle and, with their relatively modest need for exercise, fit in well with the habits and life style of elderly people. A Toy Poodle can be carried in a large handbag. This is very convenient if you use public transportation.

We have already mentioned that you need to have time and patience if you are going to own a poodle. These two qualifications are necessary not only for grooming but also for training a poodle, for its daily walk, and above all for the play and display of affection without which no dog really thrives. All in all, the hobby of keeping a poodle takes a minimum of two hours a day, but this time will be spent in a most rewarding way.

Choosing the Dog

Male or Female?

There is no particular reason to prefer one sex over the other. Both males and females readily adopt a master. The claim that female dogs prefer male masters and vice versa is totally unfounded. Nor is it true that females are generally more gentle than males. As far as character traits go, dogs are very much like people. Poodles are individuals, and generalizations about them tend to be wrong.

If you decide in favor of a male, you will have to be a little more patient when you take him out for his walks than if you had a female. He will have

Poodles are high spirited and love exercise. Their daily walk should be at least an hour long.

to do a lot of sniffing and raise his leg repeatedly to mark territory. If he catches a whiff of a female in heat, you will need extra patience and understanding for the restless behavior prompted by the natural instinct to procreate. During these periods he will tend to roam. This will expose him to greater dangers, such as being run over or, in the country, possibly being shot. After a few days, when this "state of emergency" is over, your dog will calm down again.

If, on the other hand, you have chosen a female, you should be aware that she will be in heat for a few days twice a year. If you do not want her to have puppies, you will have to watch over her with an eagle eye during these times, because her suitors will lurk everywhere and be most persistent.

If you buy your puppy from a breeder you can be sure that it will be physically and psychically healthy.

Puppy or Grown Dog?

It is a lot of fun to watch a puppy grow up and see it move gradually from the cute playfulness of a young animal to the dignity of a well-trained dog. But bringing about this change requires a considerable amount of time, effort, and patience, for everything you take for granted in a grown dog has to be painstakingly taught to the young animal. And that is no mean task.

If you consider getting a grown dog as a housemate, you should realize that it will already be fully shaped and that your influence on it will be minimal. You also do not know whether the dog has really forgotten its previous master and is willing to accept you as its human associate. Still, many of these "second tries" work out extremely well for both parties. And there are a lot of unwanted dogs that need people to offer them loving care and homes where they can live happy lives.

Purebred Poodle or Mixed Breed?

Any purebred poodle comes with papers denoting its identity and background. This documentation, which may list the dog's ancestors three generations back, is an excerpt from the stud book and is called the pedigree. If you purchase a poodle with a pedigree you can therefore be assured that you have a purebred dog that is registered in the stud book.

If you do not care much about your canine companion's lineage, you may be just as happy with a "Pomeranian

8

Poodle" or some other poodle mixture. The emphasis here is on "may," for nobody can predict with any degree of accuracy what kind of dog will develop from a charming little mongrel puppy of unknown ancestry. But it is certainly true that puppies of mixed breeds can turn out to be surprisingly intelligent dogs.

When and Where Should You Buy Your Dog?

If you have decided to buy a puppy, the right time to get it is when the litter is about eight to ten weeks old. Before that time, the puppies still need the safety and care of their mother, but by about eight or ten weeks, they no longer depend entirely on their mother for nourishment. They have started eating solid food from a dish, and no digestive problems are likely to occur when the puppy is transferred to its new home and owner.

Because of the great popularity of poodles, the yearly supply of puppies is huge and often bewildering. Serious breeders, reputable pet stores, animal shelters, advertisements in papers, as well as (unfortunately) "mass producers" and mail order firms interested only in profit, all offer "first-class champion puppies," sometimes at "sensationally low" prices. You therefore need a good deal of discrimination in selecting a puppy.

Be sure, first of all, to examine carefully any animal you consider buying.

Check the housing and the general state of health of the puppies and, if possible, of their mother. Do they look well? Are they dewormed? Have they had all the necessary vaccinations? (See "How to Recognize a Disease," page 40). If you care about having a pure-bred dog, ask to be shown the pedigree.

What a happy moment for an abandoned dog when you pick it and it will once again have a home.

Visit the puppy you think you want to buy several times, talk and play with it, and pet it. Watch its reactions carefully. Is it inquisitive and eager to play or is it reserved, shy, or even fearful? The first kind of behavior is normal, while the latter signals a behavioral disturbance due to some constitutional weakness that is recognizable as early as at six weeks and that may be permanent.

11

Considerations Before You Buy

To help you decide what kind of poodle is right for you, we will summarize here the most important information once more: Poodles are divided into three categories by size. This classification and the general appearance and bodily proportions of poodles are laid down in the "Official Standards" of the AKC (page 66).

Poodles love their sleeping baskets. But remember when you buy the basket that the grown dog will have to have enough room in it to be comfortable.

Equipment and Housing

Before your four-legged companion arrives you should visit a pet store specializing in dog accessories and get all the things you will need to take care of your dog. You will be amazed at the number of items on display there. The assortment will range from elegant "walking suits" to luxury beds. For the dog who has everything, there are dress collars made of gold, slippers, and dog chocolates, to mention just a few "essentials" for keeping a dog in style.

In the United States, there are about ten million registered dogs, and one million of them are poodles. There is obviously a lucrative market that tempts many entrepreneurs to design and offer for sale products that may or may not be necessary. To help you restrict yourself to the basics, we suggest that you limit your purchases to the following list.

Check List for Dog Accessories
- A lined leather collar or harness.
- A leash (normal length) for daily walks.
- A long leash (those with a mechanism for automatically rolling up extra line are most practical) for longer walks and for training a young dog.
- A sleeping basket long enough to accommodate a full-grown dog stretched out full length. Most dogs like enclosed baskets, but open ones are easier to keep clean.
- A pad (those with washable covers equipped with zippers are most practical). The pad should be warm but not too soft. A blanket will do, but whatever you use as a pad, make sure it is easy to clean.
- Food dishes. You need two of these, because the dog should always have fresh water available. For dogs with hanging ears, there are especially de-

Considerations Before You Buy

signed dishes that are narrower at the top than the bottom and thus prevent your poodle from getting his freshly-combed ears splattered at mealtimes. There are also useful racks available to hold the two dishes in place next to each other.

For young poodles that still pull impatiently on the leash it is best to use a lined leather collar or a harness.

- A metal comb and a brush. If you tell the dealer at the pet supply store that you want grooming implements for a poodle, he will show you the ones best suited to your needs.

You will find more detailed descriptions of grooming tools—particularly if you intend to bathe, trim, and style your poodle yourself—in our special chapter on this topic (page 56).

A Place for the Bed and a Place for Meals

Every dog needs a resting place where it feels comfortable. Choose a spot for the bed that is out of the way and free of drafts but from which the dog can watch what is going on. After all, it is a member of the family and likes to be in on everything.

Your dog should always get its meals in the same place. Kitchens and bathrooms generally have floors that are easy to clean and are therefore practical feeding places. If a little food gets spilled occasionally, it is no tragedy.

Dogs are creatures of habit with an amazingly accurate sense of time, and they are as bothered at frequent changes in routine as most humans are. That is why you should set everything up the way you plan to keep it, from the very beginning. Your poodle will appreciate your thoughtfulness, and the task of training will be much easier.

Basic Rules for Keeping and Caring for a Dog

One of the reasons that the poodle has been held in such high esteem for so long is its talent for learning. Their intelligence and eagerness to learn have earned them the reputation of being the most easily trained of all dogs. But the greatest gift will lie idle if the learning instinct is not awakened and developed early on. Do not let yourself be so charmed by the cute little fur ball that you keep postponing your efforts to train it.

A dog needs firm guidance from early puppyhood. It must learn its place in the family from a master who will teach with much love and understanding but also with rigorous consistency. If you want to do the best for your dog (and for yourself as well), you must avoid all "humanizing" and pampering. Dogs have an instinctive need to be attached to "their" master (a substitute for the leader in a pack) and to subordinate themselves to this master, but they will be truly content only if they are allowed to live in a manner that is consistent with their nature.

Getting Settled—the First Nights

When we first bring the new puppy home, we take it to a sleeping place, set it down carefully in a basket, and let it sniff and check everything out in peace. If we speak gently and pet and reassure the puppy it will quickly accept the new bed. A little while later curiosity will cause it to explore the whole household and examine everything with its nose. It is not at all unlikely that the clever little rascal may, during this first inspection— much sooner than you might anticipate— discover your best easy chair or your invitingly soft bed and try to settle down there. If you do not have the heart to say "no" firmly at this point, you have lost the first contest of will by not insisting on the educational principle that there is to be one and only one place for resting and sleeping.

There is an old German proverb that says "If you lie down with a dog you will get up with fleas." Thanks to modern soaps and powders today's poodle is not very likely to have fleas, but if the contact between people and pets is too

May the dog get on the bed? This question will have to be decided once and for all on the first night.

14

Basic Rules for Keeping and Caring for a Dog

close, there is a slight danger of catching a communicable disease from a pet. If for no other reason than this, your dog should not sleep on your bed.

The very first night can be a further test of your determination to be a disciplined dog trainer. Puppies share quite a few traits with human babies. If they feel lonely, they cry. If you give in and try to comfort your puppy by picking it up or by providing something to eat, you will not have a good night's sleep for some time to come. If the puppy figures out that its master or mistress will come running as soon as the yowls are loud and persistent enough, it will use this discovery as a means of extortion from then on. That is why, in spite of all your love and empathy, you must not give in to persistent plaints. If you remain firm, the puppy will soon get used to sleeping alone at night. Perhaps you can make it easier by placing some belonging of yours that has your scent on it—perhaps an old slipper—in the sleeping basket for reassurance. This makes sense when you remember that up to now, the puppy has slept with siblings and has snuggled up against its mother. The need for a substitute for maternal warmth, at least during the period of transition, is understandable.

Housebreaking the Puppy

How should a puppy know when and where to relieve itself, if those lessons have not been taught yet? It is pointless and unjust to punish a dog that has not

been trained, if it makes a mistake and leaves a mark on the living room rug. The guilty party here is not the inexperienced puppy but the owner who has been negligent in those duties. You should take your dog out at the slightest sign that it has to go. Take him out after eating, drinking, or sleeping, or if it starts sniffing the ground or turning around in circles.

If you watch carefully for these signs during the first few days and take the dog out to the same spot, in time and at regular intervals (every two to three hours), it will not be long before the puppy will indicate to you when it needs

Young poodles learn very easily and can be housebroken without difficulty. Take the puppy outside as fast as you can at the first sign that it has to relieve itself.

15

Basic Rules for Keeping and Caring for a Dog

to go. But please be patient; only practice makes perfect. A puppy will need to urinate or defecate at least six or seven times a day; and when it happens in the right place, you should be lavish with your praise. And continue the praise later on, when your dog has learned these lessons perfectly.

When you take your dog for walks, you should not allow it to defecate in the middle of the sidewalk. Always take the dog to the side of the road so that you will not evoke the justified ire of others, an ire that will ultimately be directed at all dog owners. In the city, where streets are rarely bordered by grass and trees, your dog will have to make do with the curb. The license fee you pay for your dog in no way relieves you of the obligation to be considerate of other people. Many urban and suburban communities have pick-up laws.

General Grooming Tasks

Care of the Coat

We have mentioned before that the condition and care of the coat is not as crucial in any other breed as it is in poodles. Regular and thorough combing and brushing, preferably every day (but at least two or three times a week), are essential not only for the dog's looks but also for its comfort.

In addition, you should take your dog to the poodle parlor every five or six weeks (at least every six to eight weeks) to have its fur trimmed and thoroughly

conditioned. If you have the time and skill for it, you can learn and perform this not altogether simple task yourself. We have collected tips and tricks for this procedure from experts. You can find them in a special chapter on page 56.

Bathing

Although poodles love the water, you should bathe puppies up to the age of five months only if absolutely necessary. Dogs occasionally have a need to perfume themselves according to their own ideas of what smells good, and they love to roll around in substances we humans consider most malodorous. In such a case, the only remedy to apply to the little "stinker" is to wash it thoroughly. But please use only bubble bath liquids or dry shampoos designed especially for dogs (available at pet supply stores). Be sure to dry your dog thoroughly after the bath with a bath towel (or better yet, a hair dryer) and keep it away from drafts (see also page 58).

Checking Eyes and Ears

Everyone knows that dogs rely primarily on their noses to take in the world, but eyes and ears are equally important sensory organs, and they have to be checked frequently because they are subject to a number of problems. Deposits often form at the corners of the eyes—especially after sleeping—and must be wiped off carefully with a lint-free cloth or tissue. Examine your dog's ears regularly, too. This is best done

Basic Rules for Keeping and Caring for a Dog

during brushing and combing. A poodle's hanging ears are more subject to trouble than the pointed ears of other breeds. At least once a month, the outer ear canal should be cleaned with some cotton and mineral oil because an accumulation of ear wax can plug the ear and cause inflammation. But proceed with extreme gentleness and care. Do not use alcohol.

If your dog shakes its head and scratches its ears a lot, this may be caused by the presence of ear mites or similar parasites. At this point you have to take your dog to the veterinarian for treatment.

Care of the Teeth

Normally, if a dog has been raised on a well-balanced diet, the process of chewing alone will keep the teeth clean. But improperly nourished dogs who are given foods that are low in calcium, too soft, sweetened, or too highly seasoned frequently suffer from a build-up of tartar, from tooth decay, and from periodontal problems which can all lead to loss of teeth (see also page 34).

Various kinds of dog biscuits and rawhide "bones" help keep the teeth clean. If some tartar has begun to form, it is useful to rub the teeth with cotton soaked in lemon juice or—better yet—a three-percent solution of hydrogen peroxide. If the accumulation of tartar is significant, it is best to have a veterinarian remove it, since it can cause irritations or abscesses that may lead to loss of teeth or other complications.

Care of the Feet

If your poodle's nails grow too long, which is often the case if it does not walk enough or has too little exercise on rough ground, they have to be clipped. If you take your dog to the poodle salon regularly, this chore is taken care of in a jiffy by the experts there. If you have no experience in clipping nails, you should not attempt to do it yourself because it is easy to injure sensitive nerve endings that are hard to detect in dark-colored nails.

Sometimes little pebbles, splinters, thorns, grains of ice, or other foreign bodies get lodged between the toes. Salt that is spread on the roads to melt the ice in winter is also hard on your dog's paws. That is why it is important to check the feet regularly. Pads that are sore from running should be powdered, and cracked pads treated with vaseline. In the winter, it is a good idea to coat the pads with vaseline before a walk, then wash them in lukewarm water, dry them, and apply either baby powder or vaseline afterwards. If there are serious injuries or if you suspect acid burn, consult a veterinarian.

Ticks and Other Parasites

Ticks, which are a great nuisance for dogs, should be dabbed with alcohol, oil, or a special tick liquid (available at pet supply stores) and removed carefully with tweezers about ten minutes later. Be careful to remove this bloodsucking parasite with the head on, because otherwise the skin can become infected.

17

Basic Rules for Keeping and Caring for a Dog

There are special powders and sprays to combat other pests. If you use powder, rub it into the coat well, allow the proper amount of time for it to act (indicated in the directions of the product), and then brush out thoroughly.

Observe these rules for care and grooming conscientiously, take your poodle to the veterinarian for a checkup once a year, and make sure that all necessary shots are received. This is the best way to prevent health problems.

Daily Life with Your Poodle

His Master's Voice

"It is the tone that makes the music." This saying is particularly true for a dog's ears. The actual words you use when communicating with your poodle are not half as important as the tone of voice in which you say them. It does not take a dog long to tell praise from rebuke. Although it does not understand our language, it is quite capable of associating certain sets of sounds with specific experiences, and of learning in time to react appropriately to these sounds. The first things your puppy will learn are its name and the command "Come." It will also grasp the meaning of the word "walk" more quickly than you might have guessed. This talent for understanding, so marked in poodles, is what we rely on in obedience training. If you generally speak to your dog in a quiet and friendly tone, an occasional stern reproof if there is cause for it will

have the desired effect and will render any punitive measure superfluous.

Punishing

If you are forced to punish your dog because even a stern and forceful censure has failed to register, you will have to resort to a spanking. But do not administer it with your hand, which you want your dog to associate exclusively with positive experiences, such as petting and giving food. You should not use the leash for this purpose either, nor a hard object, since your intent is not to make the dog shy away from you or to hurt him. A loud smack—always on the rear end—with a rolled up newspaper kept handy for this purpose will be quite sufficient to produce the desired result. Keep in mind, however, that the spanking must be administered when act is committed, in order to be effective.

Another method of punishing that is particularly appropriate for puppies is to grab the dog by the scruff of its neck. Take hold of as much fur as you can with one hand without lifting up the dog and shake it as though you were trying to get all the dust out. This is how a wolf mother treats her whelps—only she uses her teeth.

Do Not Let Your Dog Beg

A properly kept dog that has been taught good manners does not beg. People who cannot sit down to a meal without being pestered by their dog's obtrusive begging have only themselves to blame. If you make a habit of feeding your dog before you eat and never offer

Basic Rules for Keeping and Caring for a Dog

tidbits from your table, you are training your dog to become an exemplary and pleasant housemate that can be present at small parties at home or even at dinner out without being a nuisance.

Lifting Up a Dog

Grabbing a dog by the back of the neck to pick it up may look "professional" but it is not. If you want to carry your dog securely and without hurting it, cradle your hand around its rib cage and use the other to support the rear end.

Play and Suitable Toys

Any dog that does not get sufficient and regular exercise will eventually become sick. After all, the dog is a

Learning can be a game. By playing "Fetch" with your dog you can train its body and memory.

ranging hunter by nature, and its body structure, legs, and joints are designed for that way of life. Our domesticated dogs, especially those that live in cities, are given little opportunity to act on their innate need for exercise and on whatever remaining hunting instinct they have. That is why we have to be sure to offer a substitute activity, namely play. Chasing after a ball, grabbing it, and retrieving it like prey is a substitute activity that approximates the poodle's original "profession" of retrieving game that was shot by hunters.

Going for a walk is important and enjoyable, but it is no substitute for more rigorous sport which exercises muscles that hardly come into play during normal activity. That is why you should reserve some time for playing with your dog every day. This play can be incorporated into the daily walk.

Apart from the game of "go fetch" (page 39), which poodles enjoy with great enthusiasm, there are other games (such as following a scent or jumping) that are well suited for training your dog's body and memory.

A dog should have toys in its living quarters, too. Whether it is a ball, a rag, or an old bone matters little to your pet as long as it stimulates the urge to play and provides entertainment. But you should check carefully the material from which these toys are made.

Plastic, rubber, celluloid, and other kinds of artificial material (including sausage casings and cheese rind) can be dangerous for your dog. Pet stores have suitable toys. Ask there for advice.

Basic Rules for Keeping and Caring for a Dog

You should also exercise caution to prevent injuries when you play "go fetch" with your dog. The wood of the stick you throw must be tough enough not to splinter or be chewed to bits. Otherwise, a piece of wood can get stuck between the dog's teeth.

The proper toy—and this may be nothing fancier than a rawhide bone—can keep your dog occupied when you have to leave it alone for a while. Dogs must be corrected, however, when they mouth or chew anything they shouldn't.

Poodles and Children

Generally, almost all dogs love children, or at least they start out that way. Thanks to their intelligence, poodles usually get along with children especially

Children who play with a poodle should always remember that dogs can get hurt.

well. But if a grown dog has had nothing but bad experiences with children, it will understandably no longer approach them with special fondness.

To make sure that the coexistence under one roof is a happy one for everyone concerned, parents should explain to their children how a dog is to be treated and repeat the explanation as often as necessary. Parents should make it clear that having a pet means not only having fun with it but also taking on certain obligations. There is no reason why the children should not share in the task of looking after a pet. Teaching a child to love animals is not just a matter of telling him to pet the doggy and play with it; the child must also learn responsibility for the animal and what it means to look after an animal's needs.

School-age children are quite capable of taking a poodle for a walk or staying home occasionally to keep it company. They can also help with the simpler tasks of grooming if they are shown how to do it properly. And there are all kinds of other little jobs they can and should regularly perform if there is a dog around the house.

Preschool children are generally too young to know how to behave with a dog. They have not yet developed the sense of what a dog likes and what might hurt it. Parents should never leave very young children alone with a dog, especially if it is a puppy.

The puppy should not be kept completely away from a baby in the family, because it might get the idea that the carefully "hidden" little human is not a

Basic Rules for Keeping and Caring for a Dog

member of the pack (family). Later, when the dog is full-grown, it may try to keep the supposed intruder out, namely by biting. Any incidents of this sort that one sometimes reads about in newspapers are almost always, if they are investigated more closely, the result of improper handling of the dog. Allow the dog and the baby to get acquainted with each other by talking gently with the dog while showing the baby. The dog may want to sniff this unfamiliar creature, which is understandable since dogs approach all things through the nose. But do not let your pet lick the baby. There is no need for excessive concern over the possible transmission of germs. With an animal that is properly vaccinated and dewormed and is well tended there is very little chance of catching a disease from it. Do make sure to take it to the veterinarian to check for parasites

A poodle and a cat that have grown up together will get along well. If they meet later in life it is not quite so easy for these two animals, with their very different patterns of behavior, to get used to each other.

and especially tapeworms about six weeks before the baby arrives.

Once your dog has had a chance to sniff and get to know the baby, it will accept the newcomer as a member of the pack and may even try to protect it. If you give no cause for jealousy, the two will get along peacefully. Children who grow up with a dog gain experiences from which they benefit for the rest of their lives.

Getting Adjusted to Other Pets

If you already have a pet, of course you would like your new poodle to make friends with it. If the new dog is still a puppy, the two will get used to each other without great problems. Just let them sniff each other, and let *them* take the initiative (always under your supervision, of course) in approaching each other gradually.

If you are acquiring a grown dog, there is more of a problem, and you have to more cautious. If the two animals' antipathy toward each other is so great that all your efforts to make them accept each other fail, you should not count on the fact that this antipathy will disappear in time and that they will learn to get along. The opposite is more likely to happen.

In the case of a dog and a cat, particularly if both are grown animals, it is questionable whether they will ever get used to each other. Even if they do, the result may be problematic because the two animals have such different—indeed,

Basic Rules for Keeping and Caring for a Dog

opposite—body languages. The misunderstandings are less likely to be caused by the extremely sociable and adaptable poodle than by the willful cat, but that is little consolation. If a dog and a cat live together under one roof long enough they may get used to each other. They take on a common "house smell" that we cannot detect and that blocks their hunting instinct. Getting a puppy and a kitten to be friends is "child's play" in both senses of the phrase. You simply relax and let the two youngsters play. A well-trained and obedient poodle will coexist with most other kinds of pets in peace and harmony.

A Second Dog

Much as a dog likes to be attached to humans, it also needs contact with its own kind. There are friendships between dogs that not only are long lasting but can also serve as an inspiration to us. In addition, two dogs living in a human community can develop more pride because they feel less like an "oppressed" minority among the dominant majority of humans. For all these reasons you may want to contemplate getting a second dog.

If the newcomer is a puppy, all will go well. Getting two grown dogs used to each other is a little more difficult. But usually we succeed if we are willing to exercise patience and absolute justice in the treatment of the two dogs. Most important of all: Always feed the two dogs at the same time and give each its own dish.

There is only one situation in which we would not recommend a second dog. That is if you already own an elderly female and consider introducing a younger bitch into the household. In such a case fights and mutual biting are common. If you insist on owning two bitches, we advise you to get two female puppies from the same litter at the same time. Twins usually get along with each other.

When Your Dog Is in Heat

Male dogs reach sexual maturity when they are about one year old and are then ready to mate at any time. Females usually have their first heat period at somewhere between eight and ten months of age. The heat lasts between three and four weeks, but the bitch is ready to mate only at the height of the heat, which generally lasts about five days. Chances for conception are best from the ninth to the thirteenth day after the onset of heat. A bitch should not be allowed to mate for the first time until her second period of heat, nor should she have a first litter after the age of four years, because complications are likely at a first birth in animals that are either too young or too old.

Because the male dog's penis reduces to normal size only very slowly after copulation, the pair will remain locked together for about fifteen minutes. Even if the mating was against your wishes, it makes no sense to separate the dogs by force because insemination will normally already have taken place. In addition, a

Basic Rules for Keeping and Caring for a Dog

forced separation can cause serious injuries in both the male and the female.

It is possible for a female to come into heat at any time of the year, but usually it happens in the spring and the fall. Her scent then draws all the sexually mature males in the area, and they gather from near and far to pay her court.

There are two ways of avoiding unwanted pregnancies apart from spaying the female, which is best performed after her first heat and before she is four years old.

- She can be given hormone injections by the veterinarian, but frequent repetition of this treatment can impair her health.

If you go for a walk with your female dog when she is in heat you have to be prepared for the advances of her admirers.

- She can be kept in isolation from all males during her periods of heat. This can be something of a nuisance, but it is surely the healthier method.

Since you still have to take your bitch out for walks, I recommend that you carry her out of the house and put her down on the ground some thirty yards away from it (keeping her on a leash, of course). If you follow the same procedure on the way back, the scent that guides her passionate admirers will not lead right up to your door. You can also buy sprays or, even better, chlorophyll tablets, which counteract the scent and are of some help in your defensive stratagem.

If you intend to breed your poodle bitch, you should join a dog club in your area (addresses on page 69). The club will supply you with the necessary documents and will gladly give you any advice you need for the upcoming event.

The Whelping

Gestation lasts an average of sixty-three days. To figure out the anticipated day of birth you simply count ahead two months and two days from the date of mating. But to be on the safe side, you should keep a careful watch from the fifty-ninth day, because the birth may come a couple of days before it is expected.

Any arrangements for the event should be taken care of well ahead of time. This includes setting up the whelping box, which should be located in a draft-free and out-of-the-way spot in a

Basic Rules for Keeping and Caring for a Dog

warm room. An infrared lamp installed overhead will provide sufficient warmth. If a whelping box (available at pet stores) is too expensive or too bulky, several layers of newspapers covered with a few soft and clean cloths can serve as a cushion. About two weeks before the estimated date of birth the dog should get accustomed to this new bed.

Restlessness and refusal to eat are signs of the impending birth. At this time, the bitch's teats become swollen and start secreting a few drops of milk. Body temperature may drop to below 99 °F (37 °C). The birth process starts with the onset of light labor pains which gradually increase into regular contractions. One to three hours later, the water breaks, and soon after, the first puppy is born. As many as six to eight or even more puppies may follow, normally at intervals of about fifteen to twenty minutes.

After breaking the amniotic sac, the mother bites off the cord and then licks and massages the newborn puppy to start it breathing. If the mother fails to perform these instinctive tasks, the human assistant must take over and tie the cord, carefully rub the puppy dry, and free nostrils and throat from amniotic fluid. Then the puppy is placed near its mother's teats to nurse.

You should take one other precaution: Discuss the impending birth with your veterinarian and jot down his telephone number. You can never be sure that unexpected difficulties will not arise. And if, for whatever reasons, you do not feel comfortable about performing midwifery services for your dog, be sure to plan ahead so you can call on a competent person. Your poodle club or the kennel where you obtained your dog will assist you in finding someone.

But anyone who toys with the idea of raising poodles should be warned that breeding purebred dogs is not a hobby to enter into lightly. It requires a great sense of responsibility, a knowledge of genetics, a lot of time and effort, and a good portion of luck to achieve the desired results. There is no lack of breeders. Many large and small poodle kennels, some more successful than others, already exist. In the interests of keeping all breeds pure—but especially the poodle breeds—we would like to issue an urgent warning against needless and indiscriminate breeding. Let us keep our present excellent poodles from being replaced by degenerate animals with nervous and structural deficiencies.

False Pregnancy

The claim that female dogs who are not allowed to have puppies are more prone to illness than other dogs is an unfounded myth. But it is true that they sometimes undergo false pregnancies that are hard to tell from the real thing. About eight weeks after a bitch has been in heat, her teats swell and produce some milk. In this state she is able to nurse puppies whose mother does not have enough milk or has died. If there are no puppies for her to take care of she will seek substitutes and gather all conceivable objects (toys or bones, for

Basic Rules for Keeping and Caring for a Dog

example) around her and "mother" them. A false pregnancy requires reassuring and understanding behavior toward the dog on your part.

Taking Your Poodle Along on Trips and Vacations

Since dogs originally lived in packs, they have an innate need for society. A domestic dog perceives the people around him as his pack, and feels at ease only in their presence. Nothing is as hard on a dog as being abandoned by his "pack." If this state of affairs lasts for weeks on end, the animal will be so unhappy that it becomes more and more apathetic and may even refuse to eat.

This does not mean, however, that you have to give up your well-deserved vacation or take your dog to a boarding kennel. Usually you just need to plan ahead, for there are many hotels, motels, and tourist homes that will permit dogs. There are even some travel offices that offer "package tours including dogs." It is just a matter of exploring the possibilities well in advance and perhaps compromising a little on where to go. If you choose a vacation spot not too far away from home, if you make sure there are opportunities for walks and hikes, and if you make all the necessary preparations, a vacation with your dog along may prove as enjoyable as any you have ever had.

Temporary Adoptions

If it is not feasible for you to take your dog along on a trip, there is, in some cities, a less well-publicized alternative to boarding kennels. Some dog clubs and shelters collect addresses of people who are willing to adopt someone else's pet for the period of its master's absence. If you obtain such a list, you can then contact potential dog sitters and discuss terms with them. Another possibility is that the kennel where you bought your puppy might be willing to take it in while you are away. Most breeders we know are willing to take vacation guests on this basis.

Trips by Car

A dog's place in a car is in the back seat. It may look cute to see his ears flap in the wind as he sticks his head out of the window of the moving car, but he is likely to pay for the fun with conjunctivitis, tonsilitis, or an ear infection. There should be no need to mention that periodic stops are necessary for the sake of exercise and for the dog to relieve himself. Longer trips should be broken up by longer rest stops.

If your dog is not yet used to long trips and tends to vomit in the car, you can prevent carsickness by giving it a pill, such as Dramamine—available at drug stores—before you take off. Often half a pill will be enough, and if given in the morning, it will be effective all day.

Travel by Train and by Air

Your dog may be permitted to accompany you when you travel by train. Some railroad lines do not accept dogs at all, but others may have specific

*Above: Two young Miniature Poodles and a Toy ▷
Poodle. Below: For protection against the cold,
clipped poodles need clothes like the ones these
Miniature Poodles are wearing.*

*For a Toy Poodle, you can buy very practical
travel handbags with a window for the dog to see
through.*

regulations dependent upon the size of
the dog. It is a good idea to inquire
ahead of time about acceptance and
whether your poodle is considered a
large or a small dog.

If you plan to travel by air it is best
to consult the airlines in question about
their regulations for pets. In some cases,
a small dog is considered hand luggage
and travels free. Large dogs in their carriers are placed in pressurized cabins of
the luggage compartment. Some airlines
charge a certain percentage of the air
fare per pound of weight. Dogs are
usually not permitted on charter flights.
You can see how important it is to ask
well ahead for detailed information
from airlines, travel offices, or tour
organizers.

Necessary Items for a Trip

- Required documents for travel abroad
  with your dog may be obtained from
  the appropriate state agency. Keep in
  mind that requirements for entering a
  foreign country may vary greatly, depending on your destination. Generally speaking, however, you will need
  a health certificate, issued upon re-
  ceipt of a statement from your veterinarian regarding your dog's health,
  dated within the previous ten days,
  and a list of required vaccinations
  given within the past year. It is also
  advisable to check with your travel
  agent for specific airline requirements,
  too.
- Food and water dishes (do not forget
  to take a bottle of water along on
  trips!)
- A sleeping pad or basket (collapsible
  travel beds are very useful on trips)
- A leash and, where there is danger of
  rabies, a muzzle
- Dog comb and brush and, if necessary, disinfecting powder
- A first-aid kit (ask your veterinarian
  to make one for you or tell you what
  it should include)
- Canned or dry food if dog food will
  not be available at your destination. If
  your dog is not accustomed to commercial dog foods, dry or canned, get
  him used to them before the trip by
  substituting increasingly large amounts
  for the usual fare.

Specific regulations governing the
entry of animals to various countries can
be obtained from automobile clubs, the
consulates of the countries in question,
or your veterinarian.

The Proper Diet

Home-Prepared or Commercial Food?

Dog owners and experts are divided on this question. The introduction of ready-made dog foods has split the community of dog lovers into at least two camps, the conservative believers in fresh food only and the progressive advocates of commercial feeds. Your decision will be determined not only by the issue of nutritional value but also by the consideration of how much time and money you want to spend.

Since dogs were originally predators, fresh meat is the basic element in their diet, although they eat carrion as well. The wild ancestors of our domestic canines ate not only the muscle tissue but also relished the partially digested contents of their herbivorous preys' stomachs and intestines. In this way, they absorbed sufficient amounts of the vitamins and minerals that are essential components in a balanced diet for "civilized" dogs, too.

Composing a dog's daily fare that will contain the proper amounts of different foods, vitamins, minerals, and trace elements requires specialized knowledge and experience that are beyond the scope of many dog owners. We therefore recommend, especially to novices, combining a high quality commercial food with some fresh foods. This will add up to a complete diet that keeps the dog healthy and appeals to his appetite. This way you cannot go wrong. Modern canned dog food contains all the necessary nutrients. You can add roughage and fresh sources of vitamins in the form of raw, grated fruits and vegetables as well as other things like raw eggs, as needed. A dog can use carbohydrates but does not need them, and by limiting their quantity in your supplements to commercial food, you can help your dog stay slim.

If you decide on an exclusively home-made diet for your dog, you have to pay more attention to the proper nutritional composition of meals. If you think that only the best tidbits from the butcher shop will do for your pet, you are wrong. Excessive amounts of heart, liver, or prime cuts of beef are much too rich for the dog's system. The result will be obesity, which interferes with important physical functions and can cause circulatory problems and early death. The fat content of dog food should not exceed twenty-five percent.

There remains one more important question to consider: should you give your dog raw or cooked meat? Nutritionally, there is no difference. The proteins and fats contained in the meat will be absorbed in either case. Why, then, do more and more veterinarians suggest that dogs be given only cooked meat? The reason is that in recent years cases of Aujeszky's disease—a virus infection that is communicable but not dangerous to humans—have occurred with enough frequency to give cause for alarm. This disease, which is often present without visible symptoms in older pigs, generally goes undetected when these animals are sent to slaughter. If meat from these pigs is fed raw to a

The Proper Diet

dog, the disease is immediately transmitted, and since there is not yet any effective treatment for it, the dog dies within a day or two.

Raw meat may transmit not only this insidious disease but salmonella as well. This danger is greatest if meat scraps, especially from tripe, are fed. Salmonella infections in dogs up to six months often result in death. Older animals generally survive the infection without its being noticed but sometimes pass it on to people. Apart from the viruses and bacteria it may contain, raw meat can also transmit *parasites*. The larvae of tapeworms are prevalent around the mouth in beef animals and can cause severe intestinal infections if a dog eats raw meat from that area. Meat, such as heart, that has not been thoroughly bled can give rise to diarrhea if eaten raw.

You can avoid all these dangers if you feed your dog only commercial dog food of high quality. There are four different kinds on the market:

- **Canned food** provides a complete diet with all the necessary nutrients. It consists of a mixture of meats (muscle meat, tripe, heart, liver, and lung) and grains (rice, rye, oats, wheat, or corn) and contains all the important vitamins and minerals.

  Although a predator by nature, a dog can absorb carbohydrates as well. Dog food companies therefore market **two kinds of canned food**: one that contains a mixture of meat and carbohydrates, and another that consists primarily of meat or proteins. This latter type is suitable for mixing with up to a third of whole grain cereals, cooked rice, or cooked potatoes.
- **Semimoist food** is also nutritionally complete. Here the moisture content is about twenty-five percent, or about halfway between canned and dry food. Semidry dog food has a higher energy content than canned food. The need for liquid is covered partly by the moisture in the food and partly by drinking water. Since dry, semidry, and semimoist foods all contain less moisture than canned dog food, you have to be especially conscientious about supplying your dog with fresh drinking water.
- Your poodle may also be fed **semidry** or **dry dog food**. The main difference in all of these products is that in dry food, the moisture content has been reduced to between ten and twenty percent. Canned dog food, by contrast, contains about seventy-five percent water, the amount naturally present in the plant and animal products used. The food value per volume is consequently much higher in dry and semidry feeds.

Commercial dog food of these various types offers many advantages, but there are some dogs (particularly sick ones) that do not like it or with whom it does not agree. In these cases, home preparation of the dog's food is necessary.

On the following page you will find a chart that can be used for both methods of feeding. It is meant as a guideline for normally active dogs.

The Proper Diet

Feeding Plan for Poodles, Including Suggested Amounts of Food and Calories

Weights for food are given in ounces followed by grams in parentheses.
(1,000 kilo calories = ca. 4,200 kJoule)

	Weight lbs (kg)	Energy Requirement per day kJoule	Canned food* alone	Canned food with additions			Fresh food		
				14 oz cans*	+additions	Menu	Meat**	+additions	Menu
Puppies									
5th–6th week	4.5–6.5 (2–3)	1930–2600	16 (440)	1	+2 (50)	A	14 (400)	+2 (50)	D
7th–8th week	4.5–6.5 (2–3)	1930–2600	16 (440)	1	+2 (50)	A	14 (400)	+2 (50)	D
3rd month	6–9 (3–4)	2600–3260	22 (620)	1 1/4	+4.5 (125)	B	18 (500)	+3.5–5 (100–150)	E
4th month	14–15 (6.5)	4620	35 (1,000)	1 3/4	+7 (200)	B	25 (700)	+7–9 (200 + 250)	E
5th month	19 (8.5)	5670	42 (1,200)	2	+11 (300)	B	28 (800)	+9–11 (250–300)	E
6th–12th month	change over to adult feeding			1 3/4	+6 (180)	C	25 (700)	+5–7 (150–200)	F
Grown Dogs									
Toy Poodles	ca. 9 (4)	ca. 1800	—	3/4–1	+up to 2.5 (60)	C	12–14 (350–400)	+2–3 (50–80)	G
Miniature Poodles	ca. 33 (15)	ca. 4200	—	ca. 2	+up to 5 (150)	C	21–28 (600–800	+3.5–7 (100–200)	G
Standard Poodle	ca. 48–62 (22–28)	ca. 5300–6500	—	ca. 2 1/2	+7 (200)	C	28–35 (800–1,000)	+5–9 (150–250)	G

*Always feed canned food at room temperature, never straight from the refrigerator.
**Frozen meat must be completely thawed and should be warmed to room temperature. It is best to cook fresh meat.

The additional food is absolutely essential. Consult your veterinarian about the addition of calcium, phosphorus, vitamins, etc. As a matter of principle, all puppies need additional calcium from the time they are weaned until they are fully grown. This is important not only for the health of the teeth and bones but also as an aid to digestion.

The Proper Diet

Feeding Times

Age of Puppy	Feedings per day	First meal	Last meal
5 weeks	5	7 A.M.	7 P.M.
4 months	4	8 A.M.	6 P.M.
5 months	3	8 A.M.	6 P.M.
6 months	2	9 A.M.	5 P.M.
8 months	2	9 A.M.	4 P.M.

When the dog is one year old, it can be fed either once a day, preferably at noon, or the ration can be split into two meals, one to be given at noon, the other no later than 5:00 P.M.

As we have already said, these tables are nothing more than guidelines. It is impossible to indicate exact amounts because they depend on so many factors —age, weight, and sex of the dog, extent of physical activity, time of year, and also whether the dog's system makes efficient use of the food. The figures given in the tables apply to male dogs; females, which are generally a little more delicate, need somewhat less food.

Important: Do not forget to include the tidbits given as rewards for good behavior when calculating the daily food consumption.

Supplemental Food to Be Used along with Canned Food
(For total amounts, consult table on page 31.)

Menu Plan "A"
Small amounts of dry milk or cottage cheese. Thin oatmeal, lightly cooked carrots or spinach, mashed banana. One egg yolk per week. As rewards: bits of cartilaginous meat, a little dry food, or dog biscuits.

Menu Plan "B"
Oatmeal or rice mixed with half milk and half water. Cooked spinach, grated carrots, finely chopped lettuce, or half a grated apple. One tablespoon of honey and one or two egg yolks per week. As rewards and to keep the teeth healthy: dog biscuits, dry bread crusts, or bits of cartilage.

Menu Plan "C"
Cooked rice, raw oatmeal, or wheat flakes. Lightly cooked vegetables (but no cabbage, beans, or peas), parsley, grated carrot, or half an apple. One egg yolk per week. As rewards: dry food or dog biscuits.

Menu Suggestions for a Home-Prepared Diet
(For total amounts, consult table on page 31.)

Menu Plan "D"
Hamburger, finely ground veal, or chopped chicken giblets. Thin oatmeal, dry milk, or cottage cheese, and occasionally some meat broth. Lightly cooked carrots or spinach; also finely grated raw carrots and occasionally a little garlic. Mashed banana. Add some fat in the form of sunflower oil. For roughage and to absorb excess liquid, sprinkle some uncooked cereal flakes

The Proper Diet

over the food. In the winter, one table-spoon cod liver oil. Rewards as in "A."

Menu Plan "E"
Finely cut veal, lean beef, or heart lightly boiled (include the broth). Oatmeal or rice with grated carrots, finely chopped lettuce, or half a grated apple. Mix in uncooked, rolled grain to absorb liquid. One pinch salt. In the winter, add one tablespoon cod liver oil. For puppies over ten weeks old, the addition of a mineral supplement is recommended, and after twelve weeks, you may add a little glucose or honey. Rewards as under "B."

Menu Plan "F"
Beef, heart, tripe, cartilaginous meat. Once a week, some lightly cooked liver. All kinds of vegetables (except cabbage, beans, and peas), lightly cooked. A raw carrot or half an apple grated. One egg yolk per week. Some cottage cheese with a little honey or glucose mixed in every day. Mineral supplement as under "E," and rewards as under "C."

Menu Plan "G"
Beef, heart, tripe, trachea, mutton. Liver only once a week. Cooked rice, oatmeal, or rolled wheat (also uncooked to absorb liquid) with grated carrot, spinach, lettuce, or grated apple. A pinch of salt. Occasionally some cottage cheese. No more than two or three eggs a week. To chew on, a rawhide bone or, if the dog will take it, a whole raw carrot. Rewards: a little dry dog food or dog biscuits.

Amounts of Food

For Toy Poodle Puppies use about half the amounts indicated for puppies in the feeding plan.

For Standard Poodle Puppies use about double the amounts indicated for puppies in the feeding plan.

Fasting Days and Diet for Overweight Poodles
As soon as a grown dog shows any sign of obesity, you should impose one day of fasting per week. Of course, you should not plan any unusual and excessive activities for that day. And remember, fasting does not mean going without drinking! A dog should always have

If you give your dog tidbits from the table in addition to its own meals, do not be surprised if it puts on weight.

The Proper Diet

fresh drinking water available. If your poodle does not slim down under this regimen, you will have to cut down the rations—especially the carbohydrates in the supplemental foods—and at the same time provide more exercise.

If the battle is still not won, you will have to resort to a strict diet; start by reducing the total amount of food by ten percent and cut it down by another ten percent the following week. Perhaps even a third cut will be necessary. You will be able to tell without difficulty when your poodle starts getting back in shape, but check by weighing the dog to be sure. On no account should you, when the goal is reached, start increasing the daily rations, not even by one extra little tidbit! To get rid of the last fat cushions and to keep your poodle in permanent trim, you should keep increasing the daily walks.

Rations for an Aging Dog

An old dog may eat less on its own. Its diet should therefore be high in proteins and somewhat lower in fats and carbohydrates. The decrease in calories needed is usually put at about ten percent. A dog more than five years old should no longer be given bones.

Feeding a Fully Grown Dog

When the skeleton of a dog ceases to grow, the dog is full grown, and is fed only once a day or, in exceptional cases, twice. Noon is the best time for feeding. If for some good reason the daily ration has to be served in two meals, the second one should be given no later than around 5:00 P.M. On the average, small breeds reach full growth at about twelve months, large dogs at around eighteen to twenty-four months. Sometimes a sudden decline in appetite signals that the dog is fully grown. If lack of appetite persists for some time, and especially if it is accompanied by diarrhea, constipation, or vomiting, the dog should be taken to the veterinarian.

Important Feeding Rules

Your dog's meals should always be served at room temperature. Do not give anything straight out of the refrigerator or too hot. Leftover food should not sit around for hours to sour and breed bacteria. Always have fresh but not too cold water available for your dog.

To keep the teeth and chewing muscles in good shape, your dog should occasionally get a bone (not for dogs over five years old!) or a dog biscuit. Rawhide bones are also good. Teething puppies should not be given bones but dry dog food or not too hard dog biscuits, preferably as rewards for good behavior.

Dogs need a rest period after eating. Plan your walk before the meal or else an hour after it, at the earliest. Give the last meal of the day in the course of the afternoon so that your dog will have enough time to empty its bladder and bowels before bedtime.

Training Your Poodle

Education is a necessary part of growing up for animals as well as humans. Like a child, a young dog has to learn in order to get along successfully in life.

Among wolves, the wild ancestors of our domestic dogs, the pups are trained by their mother, and the whole pack follows the strongest and most intelligent member, the wolf leader. There is thus a strict hierarchy within each pack to which all members subordinate themselves unquestioningly.

You have to serve as both teacher and leader to your poodle. For this role you need authority, which you acquire not by meting out punishment but by treating your dog with consistency, love, and patience. This is the only way for you to be recognized as "leader of the pack" by your dog, and it will thus naturally obey your orders. An eight-week-old puppy goes through a process of so-cial integration and will keep trying to test and break the limits of what is permitted. Your praise and rebuke will indicate what is permissible and what is not. Even at this early stage you should be absolutely clear about your decisions and stick by them. Do not permit today what you forbid tomorrow. This is the time to housebreak the puppy and show it where to sleep at night and where to play during the day. Help your puppy by being patient and giving a lot of praise. Between four and six months, as its strength grows, it will test your authority again. During this stage of adolescent rebellion, it feels cocky enough to try to upgrade its place in the family. Again and again you will have to make it unmistakably clear that you are the stronger of the two. Grab the rebellious youngster by the scruff of its neck during such contests of will—as the lead wolf would do—and shake it vigorously. The puppy will show its readiness for submission by lying on its back and exposing its unprotected throat.

Disobedience is the result of improper training. Sometimes badly trained dogs bite; occasionally they will even bite their own masters.

Scold your puppy immediately when it makes a "mistake"; otherwise it will not grasp the connection.

Obedience Training

A well brought-up dog not only has good manners but has also learned how to behave to avoid the dangers that lurk everywhere. Just think of the heavy traffic on our streets and how quickly a disobedient dog can get hit or cause

Training Your Poodle

major damage by crossing a road at the wrong moment. Even in the country, disobedient dogs are in danger. There are usually no leash laws, but the rule that a dog has to be "under control" at all times still applies. Do not let your dog run free on walks until you are sure it has learned to respond promptly when you call or whistle.

Hitting a dog is never a good way to train it; on the contrary, it could make him shy of you or even cause biting. Some poodles feel punished if nobody pays any attention to them for a while or if they are locked into a room by themselves for a bit. In other cases a word spoken in a serious tone of voice, a firm rebuke, or a light spank on the rear with a rolled-up newspaper will do the trick. For a very young puppy, shaking by the neck, as described previously, is the most suitable and effective method of punishment.

You do not necessarily have to resort to a smack with a folded newspaper. The right tone of voice when you scold your dog is much more important.

A dog's "basic training" (i.e., what he needs to know for everyday life in the family) should be initiated as soon as the puppy joins the household. Your "pupil" should have mastered the following accomplishments by the time he is full grown.
- It must be completely housebroken and respond to its name.
- It must understand and obey the commands "Come," "Sit," "Stay," "Lie down," "Stand," and "Stop."
- It must be able to heel without pulling on the leash.
- It must be well-mannered at home as well as in strange places.
- It must behave with restraint during trips by car as well as by public transportation and may never leave a vehicle before hearing the command to do so. Always keep it on a leash when traveling.
- It must not be allowed to beg and should not accept tidbits from strangers.

Obeying Commands

"Come," "Sit," "Stay," "Lie Down"
Learning to obey the command "Come" is the first and most important lesson. Use an especially long leash with which you can pull your "student" toward you after you have said "Come." If you always follow the exercise with a word of praise, reinforced at first with a little goody, the dog will soon get the idea that it should obey the command and

36

come to you. Keep practicing even when there is no longer any need for the leash.

If it does happen that your dog goes off on his own and later returns exhausted but happy, you should not give in to your feelings of outrage. This is no time for spanking because it would think the punishment was for *coming*, something for which it has always received praise before. The fact that it has been disobedient and has run away lies too far back for its dog memory. If you want to stick to your educational principles now—and we advise you to do so—you will have no choice but to praise the guilty party for returning. It may not always sound convincing, but punishment makes sense only when it is administered *immediately* following the misdeed.

When you can rely with absolute certainty on your dog's obeying your commands you will have control over it in any situation. But until you get to that stage, you should never make the mistake of running after it and calling. This would only encourage the dog to keep going, since it can see and hear that you are following. Try the opposite instead; start walking away. Your dog will stop immediately, watch you intently, and, if you keep going, run back to you. If you make good use of this canine "pack instinct" and praise your dog for coming, repeated practice will produce the desired result. But do not go on to the next lesson until it has mastered the first one perfectly.

To teach the command "Sit," use a short leash and hold it tightly enough that the dog is forced to keep its head

Whatever you have not taught your dog when it was young and absorbed things easily, it will have to learn later, and this will require more work on its part and more patience on yours.

up. While you say the command, your free hand pushes the dog's rear toward the floor so that it has no choice but to sit down. The "Stay" command merely instructs your dog to remain in a sitting position until released.

Follow the same procedure with the command "Lie Down." The only difference is that you push down both at the neck and the rear to make the dog lie down. Here, too, of course, praise is an essential part of practice. It pays off because it keeps the dog interested in learning. If you practice these two lessons two or three times a day without displaying any impatience, your dog will soon master them.

"Stand," "Stop," "Heel"

If you have to put your dog on the leash to cross a dangerous street or for some other reason, the command "Stand" is useful. To teach it, you keep the dog close to you on a short leash, then say "Stand" and simultaneously pull up on the line to stop the dog and force it to stand still. As a further aid—and to keep it from sitting down, which it should only do when told to "Sit"—you place your free hand lightly under the lower abdomen. This will teach your dog to stand properly on command. If, once again, you are generous with praise and rewards, the dog will catch on soon and do what it is asked.

The command *"Stop"* or *"No"* is used whenever a dog is supposed to let go of something or stop whatever it is doing. If your dog is racing around wildly or barking at the top of its voice, or if you want it to relinquish a ball or a sharp bone, you call out loudly and firmly "Stop!" Your dog has to learn to obey this command promptly and reliably. You must never permit it to resume the activity after responding briefly to your command; otherwise the dog will never grasp its meaning, and all the training will be in vain.

For teaching a dog to *heel*, it is best to use a choke collar. This collar may be made of leather or of smoothly finished chain links that glide easily through a ring. For the success of this exercise it is important that the dog clearly feel it when you yank the collar back. To practice, walk your dog holding it loosely by a short leash on your left. A quiet path bordered by a hedge or a wall works best. This way the dog cannot cheat by veering off to the left. Now you say "Heel" in a somewhat drawn-out tone. Initially this does not mean anything, to

the dog, of course, and that is why you yank the leash once briefly when the dog's head is near your left knee. Stop any attempt on the part of the dog to sneak ahead and pull on the leash. Wave a long, thin switch (willow) in front of its nose when it starts to pull, but do not ever hit the dog with it. You should spend some time every day practicing heeling until the dog catches on. At first you should not walk too fast so that the dog has no reason to pull. If this happens anyway, use the command "Sit," which your dog has already learned, and then resume the heeling exercise. Here again, consistency is the crucial element. But watch out and do not extend the individual sessions too long and overtax your pupil.

Retrieving

Since poodles have a hunting ancestry, retrieving is a favorite activity for them; it is not difficult at all to teach them to fetch all kinds of objects. If you throw a ball, your dog will happily chase it, grab it, and "shake it dead" in traditional hunting dog manner. It is not so likely to relinquish the prey right off. But it will soon learn to do so if you take the ball playfully, without the use of force, and say the word "Stop," or "No." You can get the ball away most easily when the dog loosens its grip in the course of play. Then you offer praise for letting go, and start all over. Your poodle will soon understand the rules of the game and initiate this fun activity itself.

Training Your Poodle

Poodles are among those breeds that can accomplish amazing feats of learning—such as the trick shown above.

Training in Basic Obedience and Special Skills

Any poodle owner can enroll a dog in dog obedience classes taught by experts and organized by poodle clubs or other dog or obedience clubs. Any participant who passes such a course receives a certificate listing the points achieved in each exercise. Awards and trophies are passed out as recognition and as an incentive to go on to advanced skills.

All poodles are suited for sport performance, no matter which size variety they belong to. There are three levels of U.S. performance. We urge anyone who would like to have a well-behaved dog that can be trusted in city traffic and who would enjoy contact with other dog enthusiasts to join a club that sponsors training classes (addresses on page 69).

If Your Poodle Gets Sick

Before mentioning the symptoms of diseases and disorders, we would like to give you a basic understanding of a dog's physical makeup.

Short Lesson in Canine Anatomy

The canine skeleton consists of 256 individual bones connected by both rigid and moveable joints. The point on the spine between the shoulder blades marks the *withers*. A dog's height is determined by measuring the distance between this point and the floor when the dog is standing in a natural position. The thoracic and lumbar vertebrae are articulated for maximum flexibility so that the lower spine can bend in the dog's typical curled-up sleeping position and the hind legs can reach far forward in running. The special structure of the hocks in the hind legs accounts for the various gaits common to all dogs and for their ability to jump.

The energy needed to activate the approximately two hundred fifty muscles in a dog's body is provided by the basic components of the animal's food (carbohydrates, fats, and protein), most of which is converted into heat.

Of the internal organs, the heart and lungs are especially well developed. They are the source of a dog's speed and endurance. The capacity of the stomach to expand and contract as needed makes it possible for a dog to eat a big meal only once a day. The bladder is also very elastic and permits the accumulation of enough urine to satisfy a male dog's extensive need to mark territory. A dog's most important sensory organ is its extremely sensitive nose, which serves as a kind of olfactory compass.

How to Recognize a Disease

What are the early warning signs of illness in a dog? If it refuses food, drinks a lot more than usual, acts tired and apathetic, does not like to be touched, has somewhat cloudy eyes, or if the quality of its coat changes markedly, something is clearly wrong. Do not try any home remedies but take your poodle to a veterinarian, preferably the one who administered its shots and is already familiar with the dog. You can help make the diagnosis easier by reporting the changes in behavior you have noticed.

But if it is impossible to reach a veterinarian, as on a weekend, you have to have some idea of what to do. A dog owner should have enough knowledge to recognize common dog diseases and to respond appropriately in an emergency.

A dog's coat is a clear indicator of its general state of health, and any change signals some specific disorder.

A *dull coat* can be the result of an improperly balanced diet. Perhaps the dog suffers from a deficiency in vitamins, trace elements, or hormones.

Blunt hair can indicate worm infestation, liver or kidney malfunctioning, or an infection.

Loss of hair or hair breaking off is either a symptom of old age or a result

If Your Poodle Gets Sick

of a fungus infection or parasite infestation. It can also be caused by vitamin or hormone deficiencies, eczema, kidney damage, or poisoning.

Raised fur is not only a sign of alarm and anger but also occurs if your dog is suffering from sores, abcesses, or allergies.

A warm, dry nose is not necessarily a bad sign, although in a healthy dog the nose is usually cold and moist. When in doubt, take the dog's temperature.

Continual licking of the nose can be an indication of an injury or a foreign object on the tongue, or it can be caused by a cold or a sore throat.

Sneezing and coughing may be responses to a foreign object in the nose or throat, or they may be due to a cold or to tonsilitis. If a cold is accompanied by temperature, it could be a symptom of distemper.

Chronic coughing is usually a sign of cardiac weakness in old dogs. Consult your veterinarian for appropriate medication.

Pale mucous membranes, visible in the gums and the underside of the eyelids, may indicate significant loss of blood or poisoning.

Tearing eyes may be caused by eye irritations, conjunctivitis, or a head cold. Your dog has either been exposed to drafts, or there is something in its eye. Rinsing the eye with boric acid is of no use; it is better to wipe away the discharge carefully with a clean, soft cloth or tissue to relieve the itching at least temporarily. If the tearing is accompanied by a fever, there is a possibility of distemper, and consulting your veterinarian is imperative.

If your dog keeps its *head tilted all the time*, this indicates an ear infection or, possibly, some disorder of the brain. Unusual noises and sounds of high frequencies that human ears do not perceive (produced by television, for example) also cause dogs to cock their heads. This is, of course, completely harmless.

Shaking the head may be a response to a foreign object in or near the ear, but it can also signal an inflammation of the ears which should definitely be treated by the veterinarian.

If your dog is *dragging its rear end along the ground* (this is often done on a rug), its anal region is itchy. The itching may be caused by a foreign body in the anus, by the inflammation of a plugged up anal gland, or by the presence of worms in the large intestine. The latter two conditions should be treated by the veterinarian.

Frequent scratching can be caused by external parasites. Check to see if your dog has fleas, lice, or ticks. There are powders, sprays, and bath soaps available to get rid of these parasites. A dog may keep scratching one spot because it is sore. Take him to the veterinarian before the place is scratched raw and an eczema has formed.

A swelling on the muzzle is usually the result of an insect bite (bee or wasp) and looks very serious. If the swelling does not go down soon, you should have the veterinarian take a look.

A *fever* is a sign of some sort of infection and should always be checked

If Your Poodle Gets Sick

out by a veterinarian. Signs of fever are a dull, rough coat, cloudy eyes, apathy, and noticeable increase in body warmth. A dog's body temperature is normally higher than humans'—usually 101°–102°F (38.3°–38.9°C). A fever is the body's defense reaction and should not be combatted right away. But if it persists or rises above 103°F (39.5°C), there is cause for alarm.

Vomiting does not always indicate illness. If a dog has eaten too much or too fast, or if it has consumed rich food that is hard to digest, it will sometimes eat grass to induce vomiting and thus relieve the stomach. Some dogs also vomit when traveling by car or train. In this case, one of the motion-sickness pills for humans, given before departure, will have a calming effect on the nervous system and prevent vomiting.

Frequent vomiting, especially when accompanied by fever, may indicate a serious disorder. Only the veterinarian will be able to determine whether it is a case of intestinal malfunctioning, poisoning, or even distemper or leptospirosis.

Diarrhea without fever may be treated with Kaopectate. It is important that the dog drink a lot to replace the loss of fluid. If the dog goes without food for a day, the condition will usually improve. The next day you should feed your dog some cooked oatmeal with some grated apple and two or three finely mashed charcoal pills mixed in. To make the meal more palatable you may want to add some ground beef. If the diarrhea persists for three days without marked improvement and if the dog has a fever, you must take it to the veterinarian.

Stomach upsets are not uncommon in lively poodles. Your veterinarian can give you medication that relaxes the stomach.

Excessive drinking may be caused by food that is too salty. Diarrhea and vomiting also increase the need for fluid. If none of these causes are present, the excessive drinking may be a sign of diabetes, of a kidney infection, or, in the case of females, of a uterine infection.

Dark urine may result from certain foods, or it may be the sign of a disorder.

For taking a sick poodle to the veterinarian, a commercially available sleeping basket with an opening that can be closed and locked is better than an open box.

If Your Poodle Gets Sick

Blood in the urine is always a sign of trouble. It can indicate an infection in the kidneys, the bladder, or the urinary tract. Consult your veterinarian immediately.

Blood in the stool is also a serious matter. If it occurs along with repeated vomiting, it may be a symptom of potentially fatal poisoning. You may force-feed the dog a few charcoal pills dissolved in water as a first-aid measure, but be sure to take the animal to the veterinarian without delay.

Intestinal parasites. Puppies should be not only vaccinated but also dewormed before they are sold because they are almost inevitably born with roundworms. The deworming should be done under the supervision of a veterinarian who will prescribe the medication and any necessary repetition of the procedure. Older dogs develop a resistance to roundworms and are less often plagued by them. But in the case of persistent diarrhea you should have your veterinarian analyze a sample of the dog's stool to check for the presence of hookworms, whipworms, and tapeworms.

Cramps can result from infections, acute metabolic disorders, or possible poisoning by rodent poisons or pesticides.

Muscle cramps sometimes occur as a hysterical reaction to excessive excitement.

Dislocation of the kneecap is fairly frequent in lively poodles and may be caused by a "false step" in jumping or climbing stairs. Call the veterinarian. Dr. Hollman writes on this subject:

"Some poodles cure themselves by stretching the affected hind leg far back and shaking it slightly, thus causing the joint to snap back in place. If this does not happen, only the veterinarian can help. In serious cases, an operation may be necessary."

Lameness is usually caused by arthritis in old dogs. Bruising and sprains are also possible causes, as are metabolic disorders and senility. Lameness can also be a symptom of distemper or leptospirosis.

Eczema, which is a skin condition accompanied by itching, can occur on almost any part of the body. Medication for it has to be prescribed by a veterinarian. As a precautionary measure, you may wipe the dog's mouth—particularly the lips—clean after meals to keep bits of food from accumulating and rotting there.

A *tumor* may be harmless or malignant. The quicker it grows, the more dangerous it is likely to be. That is why you should not delay in consulting a veterinarian, who can tell if the growth is cancerous or not.

False pregnancy is a behavioral disorder caused by a hormonal imbalance. It occasionally occurs in female dogs about eight or nine weeks after their heat period. When this happens, the bitch's teats swell and start secreting milk. Lots of exercise, moderation in eating and drinking, and food with a low protein content help speed up the return to normal. The swelling of the mammary glands and milk production are reduced if the teats are washed three times a day with cold water that has a little wine vinegar added to it. Applying camphor ointment twice a day also helps. If there is no sign of improvement after about ten days, you should take your dog to the veterinarian for hormone treatments.

The Most Common Serious Infectious Diseases

Anyone owning a dog, particularly a young dog, should be aware of the four most dangerous infectious diseases affecting dogs. Make sure that the puppy you are about to buy has been vaccinated against them, and be conscientious about arranging for regular booster shots at the appropriate times.

Canine Distemper

Symptoms of distemper are: fever, diarrhea, coughing, and teary discharge from the eyes; at a more advanced stage, cramps and abnormal movements.

If young dogs are affected by this vicious disease, the case is practically hopeless. But even in old dogs, distemper usually causes incurable disorders of the nervous system.

Thanks to a new vaccine, puppies can now be effectively immunized as young as two weeks old, but booster shots are absolutely essential at the age of three or four months. Then the immunity remains effective for about two years.

Infectious Canine Hepatitis

Symptoms of hepatitis are fever, inflammation of the nasal and throat cavities, diarrhea, and a noticeable tenderness of the abdomen.

This viral disease, too, can attack dogs of any age, but puppies are most susceptible. Dogs that recover from the disease may be left with a clouding of the cornea, which can lead to blindness. If treatment with serums, antibiotics, and vitamins, combined with intravenous feeding, is initiated in time, it may be successful. But the only sure protection is guaranteed by a program of vaccinations. Consult your veterinarian.

Leptospirosis

Leptospirosis symptoms include fever, listlessness, lack of appetite, and vomiting. Other frequent symptoms are weakness in the hind legs, tonsilitis, and disorders of the stomach, intestines, and kidneys. In serious cases, there may be jaundice, abnormal movements, and foul odor from the mouth.

This bacterial infection is caused by various species of *leptospira* and can be accurately diagnosed only by repeated blood tests. Yearly vaccinations offer the best protection.

Rabies

Symptoms of rabies are abnormal behavior, biting without provocation, paralysis, cramps, and weight loss.

There is as yet no effective cure for this deadly disease, and any case of its occurrence has to be reported to the

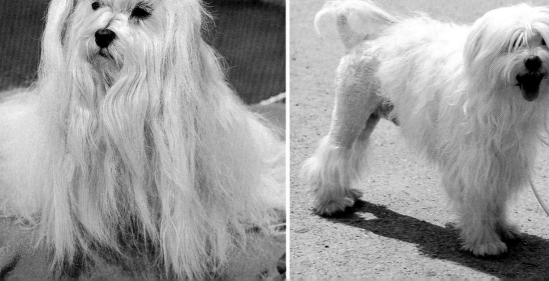

health authorities. Rabies is caused by a virus that is transmitted in the saliva of infected animals, primarily by bites. Humans, too, are susceptible to the disease. Animals suspected of having rabies must be quarantined for observation by a veterinarian. Anyone who has had contact with an animal that might have rabies must immediately receive shot treatments.

Protective immunization for puppies can be initiated at seven weeks and must be repeated at intervals of one or two years.

Combination Vaccines and Record of Vaccinations

To simplify the procedure of immunization, combined vaccines effective against distemper, hepatitis, leptospirosis, and rabies have been developed. Any of these vaccines are safe for both animals and humans. The vaccinated animals are no longer susceptible to the disease, nor can they be carriers of it.

Get in touch with your veterinarian in good time. He will advise you and will enter all vaccinations in your dog's *internationally valid vaccination certificate*. This document conforms to the regulations of international dog associations and is particularly important as a record of rabies vaccinations as well as an official proof of the dog's health and identity. You will need this document for foreign travel, and it is often required by boarding kennels. If your dog should ever be suspected of having rabies—which can happen if he has had any contact with an animal that might have the disease—health officials may ask for proof of vaccination.

Procedures of Handling that Dog Owners Should Master

To render an animal assistance you have to know how to go about it.

Taking the temperature: A poodle's normal body temperature is around 101.5 °F (38.6 °C). For Toy Poodles it is up to 102.5 °F (39.0 °C). Anything above that means a fever.

To take the temperature, insert a thermometer lubricated with some vaseline in the anus and take it out after about three minutes. You should have an assistant who holds the dog still (preferably on a table) by placing one arm around the dog's chest and holding its tail up with the other hand.

Weighing a dog is easiest if you lift the dog in your arms, step on a scale with it, and then subtract your own weight from the reading you get for both of you. The average normal weight of the different poodle sizes is listed in the feeding plan (page 31).

Giving medication in the form of pills and powders: Mix the powder with some hamburger or roll a pill into a small lump of the ground meat; then put the meat as far down the dog's throat as you can. Watch to make sure it is swallowed.

Giving drops or larger amounts of liquid: Pull one side of the lip out so that a little pocket forms, and introduce the

If Your Poodle Gets Sick

medication slowly. To keep any liquid from running out, hold the dog's head up slightly. In difficult cases, hold the mouth and nostrils shut to force the dog to swallow.

Giving a suppository is best accomplished by two people. While one holds the dog steady, pets it, and talks soothingly, the other introduces the suppository slowly as far into the rectum as possible.

Holding a dog still is essential for administering a number of treatments. The best way is to have the head rest in the

One method of checking your poodle's weight: First step on the scale with your dog, then without it. Subtract your own weight from the first reading.

crook of one arm. This leaves the other hand free to administer the treatment, pet the dog, or provide an extra secure hold. If the dog is likely to bite or has suffered a shock, it is better to use a muzzle. In an emergency, the dog's mouth can be held shut with a loop of bandaging or other material that is tied behind its head.

Providing first aid requires calmness and a clear head. Try first to reassure the injured animal in a soothing tone and get it to the veterinarian as quickly as possible. In the case of a serious accident, you should telephone ahead so the veterinarian can get everything ready to start treatment as soon as the hurt dog arrives. Surface wounds can be temporarily protected by bandaging. Do not use any powders or ointments. Injured skin can be treated with a healing salve.

In cases of *internal injuries or loss of consciousness*, do not give any liquids.

Apply cold compresses to *sprains and bruises* until the swelling starts to go down.

In cases of *poisoning*, forced vomiting can bring relief if the poison has not yet entered the blood stream. Do not feed milk to induce vomiting; use two teaspoons of salt dissolved in a little water.

Heavy bleeding may be controlled by placing a tourniquet above the bleeding wound (i.e., closer to the heart). Any strip of cloth or elastic material will do, but it has to be tight enough to stop the blood, and it has to be loosened briefly every half hour. Take the dog for treatment as quickly as possible.

If Your Poodle Gets Sick

First Aid Kit for Dogs

Any household that includes a poodle should be equipped with a special medicine cabinet for the dog. All medications, salves, powders, bandaging materials, as well as scissors and tweezers intended for canine use, should be stored separately in a place that is safe from children. Your veterinarian will be happy to suggest what should be included in the kit.

Caution: Throw out old, deteriorated items and medications past their expiration dates.

The Trip to the Veterinarian

A large, open cardboard box lined with a blanket or some similar padding is suitable for taking a sick poodle to the veterinarian. For a Toy Poodle, a carrying bag left open at the top can be used. A seriously injured or unconscious dog should be placed on his side on a blanket, which is then picked up like a stretcher. You will, of course, need assistance to do this. To keep an unconscious dog from choking to death, pull its tongue out of its mouth.

Caution: Shock and pain may cause even the tamest dog to bite.

Euthanasia

If an animal is so sick or senile or is injured so seriously that keeping it alive would only prolong its suffering, then euthanasia may not only be justified but is, indeed, the only humane solution. However, it is totally unjustifiable to destroy a healthy dog merely because the owner finds it inconvenient to keep it any longer. Old age in itself is no reason to have a dog put to sleep. With their keen noses, dogs do not depend exclusively on vision and hearing to find their way around. And dogs retain their sense of smell into very old age.

If, however, for one of the above good reasons, euthanasia seems necessary, we should not let an animal suffer one day longer than necessary. Then it is our duty to terminate the suffering by a quick death. For this we can and must take the animal to the veterinarian, so that the end will indeed be painless. All we can do at this point for our friend is to accompany it on this last journey.

Understanding Poodles

Short History of the Breed's Origin

A zoologist and an archaeologist from the University of Jerusalem have reported in the British journal *Nature* that at an archaeological site in the Jordan valley, a human skeleton about 12,000 years old was found with the bones of a young dog or wolf next to it. The human hand was lying on the animal's skeleton. The scientists concluded from this that the friendship between man and dog existed long before sheep, goats, pigs, and cows were domesticated. The taming of dogs consequently dates back more than 12,000 years. At that early date, humans must have separated some of the wild animals from their relatives, trained them for domestic use and hunting, and then bred them in captivity.

The wild ancestor of all our modern breeds, of which there are over three hundred, is the wolf. We cannot reconstruct exactly what crossings produced the poodle, which has existed as a breed for several centuries. But we do know that poodles were originally used as water retrievers and probably for herding as well. The poodle's clear liking for water is also said to account for its name, which is of German origin and derives from a word meaning "to splash around."

In any case, French and English breeders as well as German ones have all contributed to the basic type of poodle as we know it today. In 1896, a Poodle Club was founded in Munich. This club drew so much interest that branches of it sprang up all over Germany. In 1904, the organization was officially registered and changed its name to the German Poodle Club. It was responsible for formulating the first poodle standards to be recognized throughout the entire continent of Europe.

Behavioral Characteristics of Dogs

In spite of its long coexistence with man, the poodle—like all other dogs—has retained some characteristics from its wolf ancestry. As in the past, it lives as a member of a pack (now its human family) and has an instinctive need to subordinate itself to a lead animal (for which its human master is a substitute). But its behavior is not determined solely by instinct; it is also affected by environmental factors and the consequences of domestication, i.e., of man's influence on the dog. To put it simply, one could say: The less contact a dog has with humans, the more wolflike it will be in behavior. Fear of humans, competition for food, and easily triggered aggression are typical examples of such behavior.

Although poodles are one of our most intelligent breeds, the eagerness and ability to learn varies from animal to animal. But the basic patterns of behavior are the same for all individuals, as well as for all breeds. All dogs use more or less the same means of expression, or what we usually call vocal communication and body language.

Understanding Poodles

Vocal Communication

A dog's vocal expression, what we usually describe as *barking* makes use of a broad range of sounds extending from soft whining to true barking, howling, and growling, with all kinds of subtler nuances. This allows the dog to respond to each situation with a specific sound whose meaning an attentive master will soon learn to distinguish.

Body Language

Everybody knows that a friendly dog *wags its tail*. A *tail between the legs* means "I'm afraid" or "I feel guilty." These signs are clearly evident even in dogs with docked tails, such as the poodle. Other aspects of body language that involve posture are not quite so easy to interpret.

A poodle *sprawled out flat* on the floor is not necessarily suffering from heat and exhaustion. This posture can also be an expression of well-being and contentment. A *very attentive, almost overly tense posture* means one of two things: Either the dog is filled with eager anticipation, in which case his tail is wagging energetically; or, if the tail is still and the hackles are raised, the posture indicates anger that may at any moment erupt in full fury.

Facial Expression and Gestures

Facial expression is another key to what is going on inside the dog. Even the poodle, with a heavy growth of hair all over its face, exhibits many different expressions; we can usually tell by the

Waving the front paws while begging is a modified holdover from the behavior of early puppyhood.

eyes alone whether it is happy, content, grumpy, or angry.

The mouth, with the lips and tongue, also contributes to the expression of the face. There are dogs that can express their sympathy through a kind of "smile" by drawing the lips far back and showing their teeth. The tongue is used to convey love and gratitude. When our dog wants to lick us—which we should not permit for hygienic reasons—it is making a *gesture of affection* that was inherited from its ancestors. "Shaking hands" is nothing more than an elaboration of kneading (pushing rhythmically against the mother's teats with the paws), which the puppy has to do to stimulate the flow of milk. This gesture of request is taken one step further by the poodle when it stands on its hind legs or sits up on its haunches and waves its front paws to beg.

Burying a Bone

Burying leftover bones and pieces of meat is also a carry-over from the dog's wolf past. The survival of wild animals often depended on reserves of food hidden in the ground. Although our canine housemates are unlikely to experience famine, this behavior is still instinctive.

The habit of scratching the ground, sometimes even the smooth floor of a room, indicates how ineradicable the lessons of the past are and how they survive in ritualistic behavior.

Turning in Circles

Turning around several times in a circle before lying down and curling up in a ball is another habit that dates back to the ancient past. The dog's wild ancestors had to stamp down the grass to form a hollow before they could settle down into it. This exercise of walking in a circle also seems to prepare for the extreme curving of the spine that is necessary for the typical curled-up posture of a sleeping dog.

Lifting the Leg

For the male dog, marking his territory is just as important as sniffing the marks other dogs have left behind on trees, fences, lamp posts, and so on. He lifts his leg not only to relieve himself but also, and much more frequently, to leave his *scent* (little squirts of urine) to mark the territory he claims. His whole sense of self-respect would suffer if you were to deprive him of this pleasure. You should therefore allow your dog to pick up and leave such messages in an area where no one will be bothered by them.

Female dogs show no interest in these markings except shortly before and during their period of heat. They only squat to empty their bladders.

Sensory Organs

Eyes and Ears

Dogs are naturally farsighted, and their vision is primarily oriented to register movements. Although their field of vision is greater than that of humans, their normal vision is not as good as man's. Also, they see only black and white, and their three-dimensional vision is not very acute. That is why, if there is no wind to carry the scent, a dog will sometimes fail to recognize its master at a distance when he remains absolutely still.

The visual acuity of dogs varies considerably with different breeds. Greyhounds, for instance, see much better than other breeds, because following a trail with the nose (that is, with the head to the ground) would be impossible at their high speed of running.

A dog's ears are capable of hearing sounds that are inaudible to us. While the human ear registers sounds from about 16 to 20,000 Hz (sound waves per second), a dog perceives sounds from about 70 to 100,000 Hz. That is why a trained hunting dog will respond, at distances up to 500 yards, to commands from a so-called "soundless dog whistle." The whistle, however, producing sounds in the ultrasound range of about 30,000 Hz, remains inaudible for both hunter and game. This also accounts for why most of our domestic dogs are such excellent watchdogs. In addition to their sharp hearing, dogs have the ability to recognize and remember specific sounds (such as the hum of a particular car) and distinguish them from many very similar ones.

Smell and Taste

The most developed and therefore the most important of the dog's five senses is that of smell. Because their noses are so keen—far better than those of most other mammals—dogs orient themselves primarily by smell. With their very mobile and always moist noses, dogs are able to recognize substances, such as human sweat, in extremely small concentrations. Specially trained dogs, such as the ones used by customs officials to detect narcotic drugs, are even able to filter out and accurately identify specific smells in a mixture of scents.

The sense of taste, which is closely connected with the sense of smell, is also very well developed in dogs.

Sense of Touch

The network of nerves that extends over the entire body of the dog serves, among other things, to register tactile stimuli and temperature. The most sensitive areas are the front of the nose, the tongue, the lips, and the pads. Dogs also have especially modified hairs, or whiskers, that are lodged deeply in the skin (especially near the lips and in the eyebrows) and are very sensitive to touch.

Meeting Other Dogs

People who live in seclusion and avoid all contact with others begin to feel more and more insecure and turn into shy hermits or curious eccentrics. The same happens with a dog whose owner anxiously keeps him isolated from other dogs. If it is not allowed to have any

Give your dog a frequent chance to meet with other dogs. Only in this way can it learn the rules of canine etiquette that govern social encounters.

encounters with others of its kind, it will be shy, nervous, and irritable, and bite out of sheer fear.

When two dogs first meet, they usually sniff noses. Then they sniff each other's rear end and take turns lifting a leg to let the other one get a whiff to get acquainted with the smell. In the course of this ritual it will soon become apparent whether the two are likely to be friends or foes or be indifferent toward each other.

Fighting for Rank

Meetings that take place with mutual waggings of the tail indicate "we like each other." Still tails, low growling, and raised lips mean the opposite. If, in addition, the hair on the neck and back and at the root of the tail stands up, the dogs—and consequently, their masters—find themselves in a literally "hair-raising" situation. When each of the two dogs is convinced that it is superior to the other, only a fight can settle who is, in fact, the stronger. This usually looks much worse than it is, for as soon as one of the dogs gives in by lying on its back and exposing its unprotected throat to its opponent, the matter is decided and the fight over. That is how things ordinarily go, at least among normal dogs. Unfortunately there are some behaviorally disturbed animals that do not conform to the hereditary rules of canine fairness, and these dogs occasionally bite even puppies, something no normal dog would ever do.

You should never bodily interfere to separate two fighting dogs, or you may end up being the main casualty. If you step in, not only the stranger but your own dog as well may bite you in the heat of battle; and that is something you should not risk. Sometimes a diversionary tactic works, particularly if it is used before the fight starts in earnest. Almost any poodle owner knows some signal, such as the word "Cat!" or "Where is the lady?" which his or her dog finds impossible to resist. By using this trick, the dog is given the chance to get away in time without losing face by retreating.

The more contact a dog has with other dogs, the more secure it gets in its behavior toward them.

Any dog with healthy self-confidence will defend its territory—even against the mailman.

Understanding Poodles

Display Behavior

This concept originated in the study of animal behavior and refers, among other things, to how animals set up ranking orders. Display here means showing off, creating an impression of strength, pretending to be bigger, raising the fur, baring the teeth, and so on, to intimidate the opponent and cause it to retreat. Often the one who can exaggerate most convincingly succeeds in becoming the winner without having to engage in any fight to test its strength.

Behaviorally Disturbed Dogs

All reactions of a dog that deviate from normal behavior are due to psychic disorders and are called disturbed behavior. They have various sources:

- Inappropriate selection for breeding that places too much emphasis on beauty and physical perfection and not enough on keeping the strain healthy and encouraging the best character traits.
- A severe illness (such as distemper) that has led to irreversible brain damage.
- Mistakes in training and inappropriate treatment and living conditions. These errors can often be traced back to two totally different causes. One is ignorance, which should properly be called lack of interest in the animal. The other—unfortunately more frequent—cause is the irrational but deep-rooted need to see animals in human terms.

(We call this the *babying syndrome*.) This unnatural expression of affection is totally inappropriate for a dog, whose nature and character is still determined by his "wolf" heritage. No matter how well-intentioned, this kind of attitude reveals a total misunderstanding of what it means to love an animal.

As you can see, the psychic well-being of your dog depends not only on his background and on humane living conditions but also on consistent training and on your treating it in a manner that is in keeping with its canine nature.

If nobody pays any attention to a dog and it has nothing to do, its instinctual energies can build up and may find expression in aggressive behavior. The best and most natural way to get rid of accumulated aggression is to give the animal a lot of exercise in the fresh air, preferably combined with play and learning.

Clipping a Poodle and Care of the Coat

Useful Tips from an Expert

The first thing to be aware of in clipping a poodle is the difference between general grooming on the one hand and clipping and basic styling of a poodle on the other. The latter requires a considerable investment of time and effort, not to mention skill, which is why most poodle owners entrust their dogs to experts in poodle styling. The job, if it is to be done well, takes a conscientious professional about three hours. According to Mrs. Bertelmann, bathing, drying, brushing, and combing a poodle takes about an hour and a half; clipping requires just about as much time.

If you want to learn to style your poodle yourself, you should start by taking it to a poodle parlor to see exactly what a regulation poodle clip looks like (you may want to take some photos to serve as models). A detailed description of these clips follows, and then we will tell you how you actually proceed.

Standard Clips

On the continent, the FCI recognizes only two clips: the Continental and the Puppy clip. The AKC recognizes these two plus the English Saddle Clip.

English Saddle Clip

The hindquarters are scissored down to a short blanket of hair with a curved shaved area on the flanks and two shaved bands on each hind leg. Face, throat, feet, forelegs, and base of tail are shaved, leaving puffs on the forelegs and a pompon at the end of the tail. The rest of the coat is left long with only slight shaping.

Continental Clip

This style is like the English Saddle clip except that the hindquarters are shaved, leaving (optional) pompon on the hips and bracelets on the hind legs.

Puppy Clip

In this style, which is officially accepted by the AKC for dogs up to one year old, the coat is left long except for the face, throat, feet, and base of tail. The following detailed description reflects European practice.

The following parts are *shaved*:
- The front feet up to the height of the dewclaw and the hind feet up to the same height.
- Head and tail as described under the English Saddle Clip. It is sometimes permissible to leave a beard no longer than one-half inch (one cm) on the lower jaw and trimmed parallel to the line of that jaw. A goatee is never allowed. The pompon on the tail can be omitted, but this may slightly lower the evaluation for hair texture.

The hair on the following parts is *shortened*:
- The back. The coat on the back must be at least one-half inch (one cm) long. The hair becomes gradually longer over the ribs and on down the legs.

Clipping a Poodle and Care of the Coat

The following *shaping* is customary:
- Enough hair is left on top of the head to form a topknot. Also, the area extending from the topknot to the withers is trimmed to form a gradually descending line, which in turn lends a slightly conical form to the entire body shape. The line to the shaved feet must not be broken.
- The hair on the ears may be shortened from the base of the ear down to no more than one-third of the leather by using scissors or clippers in the direction of the hair growth. The lower part of the leather should be covered with hair that gets gradually longer and is feathered at the bottom. The lower ends may be trimmed with scissors.

At the beginning you will want to have your poodle clipped by a professional. Later on you may want to try it yourself with the help of the instructions in this book.

The hair on the legs is shaped into pantaloons that end neatly at the shaven feet. The thickness of the coat should increase toward the shoulders and hips to a maximum of 2 to 2½ inches (5 to 7 cm), depending on the size of the poodle. The pantaloons of the hind legs should be so cut as to reveal the angle of the joints.

There are all kinds of other trim styles, but they are not recognized at shows. The judges may allow some variation in detail.

Equipment Needed for Trimming and Grooming

- A firm table and a bathtub or large plastic tub.
- A rubber mat for the top of the table and perhaps another one for inside the bathtub to keep the poodle from slipping.
- Electric clippers of professional quality with heads No. 7, 10, and 15.
- Straight scissors about 8 inches (19–20 cm) long, preferably with fine serration that keeps the thin hair from slipping between the blades.
- A fine-toothed and a coarse-toothed metal comb.
- A special poodle brush of natural and nylon bristles or one with wire bristles set in rubber.
- A normal hair dryer or, preferably, a special dryer for dogs that is equipped with a hair filter. (Professionals also use a drying chamber.) The sales personnel in a pet supply store will help

Clipping a Poodle and Care of the Coat

you choose the model best suited for your purposes.

- A large and a small towel to rub the dog dry.
- Special dog shampoo (do not use ordinary shampoo, let alone soap!).
- Hair spray to give the coat gloss.
- Ear cleansing solution and ear powder.

Daily Grooming

You should groom your puppy's coat daily because, first of all, it is good for the coat and, secondly, the puppy will get so used to the procedure that it will later put up with the clipping patiently.

For a puppy, a thorough combing and brushing of the coat is all that is needed. Be careful not to leave any knots or matted places because otherwise the next session may be painful for you as well as the dog. A poodle puppy is brushed against the growth of the hair (but without tugging) until the hair is so smooth and pliable that the coarse-toothed comb can be drawn through it with almost no effort. A thorough combing with the coarse-toothed comb is then followed by one with the fine comb.

A grown poodle with a fully developed adult coat is first brushed *with* the lie of the fur and then *against* it. This is followed—as in the case of a puppy—by a thorough combing down to the roots of the hair. Start with the head then proceed down the back to the base of the tail, then down the sides to the legs. Next come the ears and the top of the head, where the hair is combed from the back and the front to form a topknot. The tail is last.

Clipping and Styling

Puppy Clip

- Before clipping and shaving—but after the dog has relieved itself—the poodle is bathed (in water at body temperature), rubbed dry, and dried *thoroughly* with a hair dryer. While using the dryer, brush the entire coat in the direction of the head. Then comb the hair well.
- Now take the clippers with blade No. 7 and run them from the neck down the dog's back (i.e., in the direction of the hair) and then down the sides.
- Replace the blade with a No. 10 or 15. Now place one hand under your poodle's chest and lift the animal's front up a little, while you carefully clip the stomach. If the dog is a female, be careful not to nip her teats.
- Next are the cheeks, chin, and throat. If you feel experienced enough, you can still use the clippers, but if you are new at the job you had better stick with scissors.
- Now come the jobs for the scissors. You begin by trimming the topknot into a nice, even shape. It should look elegant, flaring out a little to the front and back but merge without any visible break with the neck line and continue on down the back. Next you take the scissors and cut the hair in a

line running from the outer corner of the eyes to the ears. Make sure the base of the ear is clearly visible. After cutting both sides even, you shape the beard, which should not stick out beyond the cheekbones but should run parallel to the line of the lower jaw.

- Finally you trim the feet. Here the aim is to make the transition from shaved foot to full coat even on all four feet. Even lines are, of course, important for the entire body.
- Now, use hair spray to put the last touch on your labors.

Continental Clip
- Bathing, drying, brushing, and combing as under the Puppy Clip.
- For a preliminary clipping of the feet, use the clippers with a No. 10 or 15 head. Shave down under the toes on the front feet and halfway up the metatarsus on the back feet. The remaining hair on the toes is trimmed off with scissors.
- Use the No. 10 head for trimming the head hair, or scissor it. The front of the topknot should billow out over the eyes without hiding them. On the sides it should be full over the ears.
- Now you trim the upper and lower parts of the muzzle by working from the stop (begin at the lower eyelid) to the front of the nose and down the cheeks almost down to the Adam's apple.
- There should be only a small beard on the upper lip, and it should not stick out from the cheeks, and certainly not

as far as the ears. Its lower edge has to be trimmed in a straight line that runs parallel with the lower line of the muzzle.
- The hind legs are shaved downward to just above the hock, as are the bare parts of the front legs. Use a No. 7 head for this.
- Now take the scissors to shape the "jacket" that covers the chest and the back down to the shaven hindquarters. Cut the fur in a nice even line all around the body at the back. The line of the jacket from the back to the head should be a smooth upward curve.
- Finally, the puffs or pompons on the legs and the tail are shaped. They should all be as round and even as possible. Those on the hind legs should hug the hocks.
- Spray the entire coat, and your poodle will stand in the full glory of its new attire.

What Remains to Be Done
- Trim the fine hairs between the pads of the feet so that nothing can get stuck to them, but do not cut them back all the way (and do not trim them too far back in winter) because these hairs do have a protective function.
- Trim the hairs at the inside corners of the eyes, otherwise the tear ducts may become gummy and inflamed. Then apply an eye cream.
- After every trimming session you should carefully pluck the hairs grow-

ing inside the ear as far as the ear canal so they do not accumulate ear wax and block the ear. Clean the inside of the ears very gently but thoroughly with a Q-tip dipped in mineral or baby oil and then powder them.

- You should also keep the hairs in the anal region short to keep them from getting dirty and matted. Here is a note on this topic from the veterinarian Dr. Hollmann: "A poodle suffering from vomiting fits was brought to my office. Diagnosis: The hair around the anus was stuck together, blocking the anus!"

The Poodle Family and Related Breeds

Glossary of the Most Important Terms

Here are some of the specialized terms frequently used by dog fanciers:

Croup = Part of the body over the sacrum, the first four tail vertebrae, and the hip joints of the pelvis.

Cryptorchism = Condition where both testicles are retained in the abdominal cavity (usually present shortly before or after birth).

Dewclaw = A vestigial fifth digit that does not reach the ground.

Dock = Shortening the tail by cutting it. Originally this was done with poodles to keep their tails from getting injured while swimming and tracking game.

Harlequin = Patched coloration; in poodles, black-and-white and black-and-tan.

Hock = Tarsus, or the collection of bones in the hind leg that forms the joint which is the dog's true knee.

Jacket = In the continental clip, the part of the coat that is left long and covers the front part of the body.

Leather = The flap of the ears.

Markings = Patches of a different color in the coat of a dog.

Monorchism = Condition when one testicle is retained in the abdominal cavity (see Cryptorchism).

Muzzle = The front part of a dog's head, including the nasal bone, nostrils, jaws, and mouth cavity.

Pantaloons = In poodles, the long hair that is left on the legs as required for the Puppy Clip.

Rudder = The tail.

Stop = The step up from the muzzle to the skull.

Withers = The highest point of the shoulders where the neck meets the shoulders. The distance between the ground and this point is what is referred to as the "height" of a dog.

The Poodle (Caniche)

Our modern poodle is the result of about two hundred years of selective breeding aimed at refining the type. This work has been done by German, French, English, and, to a lesser extent, by Spanish and Hungarian dog enthusiasts. According to the FCI, France is the place of origin of this breed, the French name of which is *Caniche* (derived from *chien canard*, or duck dog). The result of crossings between shaggy shepherd-type dogs and spaniels, the poodle was first used as a water retriever in hunting. It has always been held in high esteem for its amazing talent for learning and its eagerness as a retriever. It was probably also used for shepherding in its earlier history.

Today the poodle, thanks to its attentive and sociable nature and its exceptional quickness to learn, ranks near the top in popularity among breeds kept as all-purpose house pets and companions.

In contrast to the old-style Corded Poodles, whose thick, curly hair was allowed to grow uncut, the modern poodle has to be clipped. The American Kennel Club recognizes three styles, the *English Saddle Clip*, the *Continental Clip*, and the *Puppy Clip* (see page 67).

In Europe, the FCI recognizes only two clips: a version of the Continental Clip called the Classical or Lion Clip and the Puppy or Modern Clip. The UCI also recognizes a variant of the Puppy Clip called the Karakul Clip, in which the ears are shorn and the beard is trimmed in a rounded form.

Standard Poodle

The Standard or large Poodle should look just like the more common Miniature Poodle and have all the same characteristics.
Height: Over 15 inches (39 cm).

Miniature Poodle

The Miniature Poodle, which has the broadest breeding base (although the first German poodles to be recognized by clubs around the turn of the century were closer in size to the Standard Poodle), is the most popular and most widely kept poodle today.
Height: No more than 15 and no less than 10 inches (39 and 26 cm).

Toy Poodle

The Toy Poodle should look like a smaller version of the Miniature Poodle and have the same proportions.

In order to achieve this very small size, it was necessary to cross poodles with other small breeds, such as the Maltese. Consequently, Toy Poodles are not, strictly speaking, purebred although they look like true poodles. Breeding Toys requires an exceptional degree of experience, knowledge, and skill to keep the effects of the nonpoodle breed to a minimum. Because of their convenient small size, Toy Poodles have, in recent years, increased in popularity.
Height: Under 10 inches (26 cm).

Colors: The internationally recognized colors for all three sizes are
- the solid colors—black, brown, white, apricot, and silver. The AKC also lists blue, cream, and café-au-lait.
- The UCI rules also permit black-and-tan and black-and-white harlequins.

Size: European dog clubs also define the size categories somewhat differently from the AKC. They list
- Large Poodles, or Royal Poodles: Over 18 and up to 23 inches (45 to 58 cm)
- Small Poodles: Over 14 and up to 18 inches (35 to 45 cm)
- Miniature Poodles: Over 11 and up to 14 inches (28 to 35 cm)
- Toy Poodles: No smaller than 9½ and up to 11 inches (24 to 28 cm). This European Toy Poodle is recognized only by the UCI.

The Poodle Pointer

The Poodle Pointer was created by crossing an old-style Standard Poodle with a Pointer. The intent was to breed a versatile and robust working dog for all kinds of hunting. Today, hunters like to use Poodle Pointers as lead dogs and appreciate them particularly for trailing a scent and barking to indicate downed game. The Pointer Poodle is less suitable as a general house dog and companion, particularly in cities. This strain's thick, smooth coat is not clipped but only combed and brushed.
Colors: Dark brown, light brown, and black. Sometimes small white markings are permitted.
Height: 24 to 27 inches (60 to 68 cm) for males; 22 to 25 inches (55 to 63 cm) for females.

Poodle Crossings with Wild Canines

The **Puwo** is a cross between a Poodle and a wolf bred for research purposes at the Institute for Study of Domestic Animals at the Christian-Albrechts University in Kiel (under the supervision of Professor Wolf Herre). One of the findings is that there is no genetic link between the physical and the behavioral traits that are passed on to the offspring. A dog that resembles a poodle in appearance may be shy like a wolf, while another one that looks more like a wolf may have the nature of a sociable pet.

The Kiel Institute is studying how the genealogical histories of different animals influence the changes brought about by domestication. This project is not only of theoretical interest but should also yield practical results for those engaged in breeding Poodles and other dog breeds.

The **Puscha**, which is the result of crossing a poodle with a side-striped jackal, was also bred at the Institute for Study of Domestic Animals in Kiel. In recognition of his research, the Institute's chief, Professor Wolf Herre, has been named an honorary member of the German Poodle Club.

Poodle-like Dogs

We are going to mention these breeds only in passing because they are mixtures of several small dog breeds whose identity is often impossible to determine with accuracy.

Poodle-like dogs is a collective term for the various kinds of Bichons, a very old group of poodle-like dwarf breeds with finely curled or silky-soft long hair. This type of dog originated in the Mediterranean. Today Bichons are divided into five categories depending on the texture of their hair.

Bichon Bolognais

The Bichon Bolognais comes from Italy, as its name suggests. This somewhat stocky looking but well proportioned little dog looks like a cute toy and is characterized by a very lively and devoted nature. It is a favorite (and expensive) pet of wealthy ladies. Its coat, made up of thick tufts of silky-soft curly hair, should not be clipped.
Height: Not over 12 inches (30 cm).
Color: Pure white.

Bichon Havanais

The Bichon Havanais resembles its cousin from Bologna in build and character. Its hair, which should be silky-soft and straight except for a slight curl at the ends, must not be clipped except perhaps around the muzzle. Its long-haired and curved tail is carried high; the relatively large eyes bordered by almond-shaped lids should be black or at least very dark.
Height: 11 to 13 inches (28 to 32 cm).
Colors: Dark beige to pure white; also gray or white with beige spots.

Bichon petit Chien-Lion

This is a very rare variety of the Bichon. Its name derives from the usual style of clipping which gives the dog the appearance of a miniature lion. The hindquarters are shaved with bushy tufts left on all four feet as well as on the end of the tail which is curved up over the back. The fur on the head and down the back forms a "lion's mane." The sixteenth-century English Water Dog (*Canius auiarius aquaticus*), an ancestor of the modern poodle that was also shorn lion-style, must have looked similar though larger. Like all Bichons, the Chien-Lion is a lively and amusing little fellow and makes both an affectionate pet and a good watchdog.
Height: Up to 14 inches (35 cm) for males;

The Poodle Family and Related Breeds

8 to 12 inches (20 to 30 cm) for females.
Colors: All colors are permitted, but white is preferred.

Bichon Maltais, or Maltese

This Maltese miniature dog was already known and highly appreciated in antiquity. The thick, silky hair that grows on its head reaches down at least as far as the point of the shoulder and makes the little dog appear larger than it really is.

The Maltese Bichon is loyal, modest, and lovable and is a favorite of high society. The profuse hair on its head is often kept under control with ribbons. Daily combing and brushing are absolutely essential.
Height: 8½ to 10 inches (12 to 26 cm) for males; 8 to 10 inches (20 to 25 cm) for females.
Color: Only pure white is desirable.

Bichon Téneriffe

This variety, also known as *Bichon à poil frisé*, is found primarily in France and Belgium. Its coat is made up of wooly hair 3 to 4 inches (7 to 10 cm) long that forms corkscrew curls. Like its cousins, the Teneriffe is lively, intelligent, reliable, and faithful.
Height: No more than 12 inches (30 cm).
Colors: Pure white; also with patches the color of café au lait on the ears.

AKC Standard for the Poodle

General Appearance, Carriage and Condition
That of a very active, intelligent and elegant-appearing dog, squarely built, well proportioned, moving soundly and carrying itself proudly. Properly clipped in the traditional fashion and carefully groomed, the Poodle has about it an air of distinction and dignity peculiar to itself.

Head and Expression
(a) *Skull*—Moderately rounded, with a slight but definite stop. Cheekbones and muscles flat. Length from occiput to stop about the same as length of muzzle.
(b) *Muzzle*—Long, straight and fine, with slight chiseling under the eyes. Strong without lippiness. The chin definite enough to preclude snipiness. Teeth white, strong and with a scissors bite.
(c) *Eyes*—Very dark, oval in shape and set far enough apart and positioned to create an alert intelligent expression.
(d) *Ears*—Hanging close to the head, set at or slightly below eye level. The ear leather is long, wide, and thickly feathered; however, the ear fringe should not be of excessive length.

Neck and Shoulders
Neck well proportioned, strong and long enough to permit the head to be carried high and with dignity. Skin snug at throat. The neck rises from strong, smoothly muscled shoulders. The shoulder blade is well laid back and approximately the same length as the upper foreleg.

Body
To insure the desirable squarely-built appearance, the length of body measured from the breastbone to the point of the rump approximates the height from the highest point of the shoulders to the ground.
(a) *Chest*—Deep and moderately wide with well sprung ribs.
(b) *Back*—The topline is level, neither sloping or roached, from the highest point of the shoulder blade to the base of the tail, with the exception of a slight hollow just behind the shoulder. The loin is short, broad, and muscular.

The Poodle Family and Related Breeds

Tail
Straight, set on high and carried up, docked of sufficient length to insure a balanced outline.

Legs
(a) *Forelegs*—Straight and parallel when viewed from the front. When viewed from the side the elbow is directly below the highest point of the shoulder. The pasterns are strong. Bone and muscle of both forelegs and hindlegs are in proportion to size of dog. **(b)** *Hindlegs*—Straight and parallel when viewed from the rear. Muscular with width in the region of the stifles which are well bent; femur and tibia are about equal in length; hock to heel short and perpendicular to the ground. When standing, the rear toes are only slightly behind the point of rump. The angulation of the hindquarters balances that of the forequarters.

Feet
The feet are rather small, oval in shape with toes well arched and cushioned on thick firm pads. Nails short but not excessively shortened. The feet run neither in nor out. Dewclaws may be removed.

Coat
(a) Quality—(1) curly: of naturally harsh texture, dense throughout. *(2) corded:* hanging in tight even cords of varying length; longer on mane or body coat, head, and ears; shorter on puffs, bracelets, and pompons. *(b) Clip*—A Poodle under 12 months may be shown in the Puppy Clip. In all regular classes, Poodles 12 months or over must be shown in the English, Saddle, or Continental clip. In the Stud Dog and Brood Bitch classes and in a non-competitive Parade of Champions, Poodles may be shown in the Sporting clip. A Poodle shown in any other type of clip shall be disqualified.

(1) Puppy: A Poodle under a year old may be shown in the "Puppy" clip with the coat long. The face, throat, feet, and base of the tail are shaved. The entire shaven foot is visible. There is a pompon on the end of the tail. In order to give a neat appearance and a smooth unbroken line, shaping of the coat is permissible.
(2) English Saddle: In the English Saddle clip, the face, throat, feet, forelegs and base of the tail are shaved, leaving puffs on the forelegs and a pompon on the end of the tail. The hindquarters are covered with a short blanket of hair except for a curved shaved area on each flank and two shaved bands on each hindleg. The entire shaven foot and a portion of the shaven leg above the puff are visible. The rest of the body is left in full coat but may be shaped in order to insure overall balance.
(3) Continental: In the Continental clip the face, throat, feet, and base of the tail are shaved. The hindquarters are shaved with pompons (optional) on the hips. The legs are shaved, leaving bracelets on the hindlegs and puffs on the forelegs. There is a pompon on the end of the tail. The entire shaven foot and a portion of the shaven foreleg above the puff are visible. The rest of the body is left in full coat but may be shaped in order to insure overall balance.
(4) Sporting: In the Sporting clip a Poodle shall be shown with face, feet, throat, and base of tail shaved, leaving a scissored cap on the top of the head and a pompon on the end of the tail. The rest of the body and legs are clipped or scissored to follow the outline of the dog, leaving a short blanket of coat no longer than one inch in length. The hair on the legs may be slightly longer than that on the body.

The Poodle Family and Related Breeds

In all clips the hair of the topknot may be left free or held in place by no more than three elastic bands. The hair is only of sufficient length to present a smooth outline.

Color

The coat is an even and solid color at the skin. In blues, grays, silvers, browns, café-au-laits, apricots, and creams, the coat may show varying shades of the same color. This is frequently present in the somewhat darker feathering of the ears and in the tipping of the ruff. While clear colors are definitely preferred, such natural variation in the shading of the coat is not to be considered a fault. Brown and café-au-lait Poodles have liver-colored noses, eye rims, and lips, dark toenails, and dark amber eyes. Black, blue, gray, silver, cream, and white Poodles have black noses, eye rims, and lips, black or self-colored toenails, and very dark eyes. In the apricots, although the foregoing colored is preferred, liver-colored noses, eye rims and lips, and amber eyes are permitted but are not desirable.

Parti-colored dogs shall be disqualified. The coat of a parti-colored dog is not an even solid color at the skin but is of two or more colors.

Gait

A straightforward trot with light springy action and strong hindquarters drive. Head and tail carried up. Sound effortless movement is essential.

Size

The Standard Poodle is over 15 inches at the highest point of the shoulders. Any Poodle that is 15 inches or less in height shall be disqualified from competition as a Standard Poodle.

The Miniature Poodle is 15 inches or under at the highest point of the shoulders, with a minimum height in excess of 10 inches. Any Poodle which is over 15 inches or is 10 inches or less at the highest point of the shoulders shall be disqualified from competition as a Miniature Poodle.

The Toy Poodle is 10 inches or under at the highest point of the shoulders. Any Poodle that is more than 10 inches at the highest point of the shoulders shall be disqualified from competition as a Toy Poodle.

Value of Points

General appearance, temperament, carriage and condition 30
Head, expression, ears, eyes, and teeth 20
Body, neck, legs, feet, and tail 20
Gait 20
Coat, color, and texture 10

Major Faults

Any distinct deviation from the desired characteristics described in the Breed Standard with particular attention to the following:

Temperament—Shyness or sharpness.
Muzzle—Undershot, overshot, wry mouth, lack of chin.
Eyes—Round, protruding, large or very light.
Pigment—Color of nose, lips, and eye rims incomplete, or of wrong color for color of dog.
Neck and Shoulders—Ewe neck, steep shoulders.
Tail—Set low, curled, or carried over the back.
Hindquarters—Cow hocks.
Feet—Paper or splayfoot.

Disqualifications

Clip
A dog in any type of clip other than those listed under **Coat** shall be disqualified.
Parti-colors
The coat of a parti-colored dog is not an even solid color at the skin but of two or more colors. Parti-colored dogs shall be disqualified.
Size
A dog over or under the height limits specified shall be disqualified.

Geographical List of AKC Obedience Clubs

(Reprinted with the permission of the American Kennel Club)

The following clubs are licensed by the AKC. There are additional sanctioned obedience clubs that are working towards becoming licensed, and there are also clubs that specialize in specific breeds.

Alabama

Birmingham Obedience Training Club, La Rae Stephens, Rt. 2, Box 76, Trussville, AL 35173

Huntsville Obedience Training Club, Mary Bankich, 3113 Hale Drive, Huntsville, AL 35805

Mobile Bay Dog Training Club, Mrs. Lu Jane Hill, Rt. 1, Box 25C, Fairhope, AL 36532

Alaska

Dog Obedience Training Club of Anchorage, Ms. Tonya Struble, 2981 Concord Lane, Anchorage, AK 99502

Arizona

Old Pueblo Dog Training Club, Ms. Sandy Frumhoff, 6038 East 21st Street, Tucson, AZ 85710

Phoenix Field & Obedience Club, Joan Weschler, 15 East Concorda, Tempe, AZ 85282

Arkansas

Little Rock Dog Training Club, Jean Jones, 717 North Bryan, Little Rock, AR 72205

California

Bakersfield Obedience Training Club, Shirley Taylor, 920 Stanford Court, Bakersfield, CA 93305

County Wide Dog Training Club, Ms. Dorothy Kinnaman, 879 Ludwig Avenue, Santa Rosa, CA 95401

Davis Dog Training Club, Ms. Sue Stowell, 645 Devonshire Drive, Dixon, CA 95620

Deep Peninsula Dog Training Club, Ms. Lori Miner, 745 Olive Street, Menlo Park, CA 94025

Fremont Dog Training Club, Jean Seth, 3708 Savannah Road, Fremont, CA 94538

Fresno Dog Training Club, Evelyn James, 29255 Highway 145, Madera, CA 93637

Hollywood Dog Obedience Club, Ms. Alta Beall, 1200 Manzanita Street, Los Angeles, CA 90029

Los Angeles Poodle Obedience Club, Ms. Connie Sullivan, 3480 Cudahy Street, No. C, Huntington, CA 90255

Marin County Dog Training Club, Mrs. Mid Rothrock, 8439 Elphick Road, Sebastopol, CA 95472

Monterey Bay Dog Training Club, Nancy Lewis, 208 Hecker Pass Road, Watsonville, CA 95076

Motoc Dog Obedience Club, Inc., Judy Christopher, 1322 West 6th Street, Ontario, CA 91762

Mt. Diablo Dog Training Club Inc., Melissa Holdrich, 3929 Elston Avenue, Oakland, CA 94602

Oakland Dog Training Club, Inc., Suzanne A. Harvey, 6676 Estates Drive, Oakland, CA 94511

Obedience Club of San Diego County, Michelle Roybark, 13804 Olive Mill Way, Poway, CA 92064

Orange Coast Obedience Club, Melody Murphy, 8322 Castillian Drive, Huntington Beach, CA 92646

Pasanita Obedience Club, Jeanine Jahelka, 4340 Bel Air Drive, La Canada, CA 91011

Sacramento Dog Training Club, Mark Steffens, 2824 Aurora Way, Sacramento, CA

San Francisco Dog Training Club, Catherine Knight, 1851 Monterey Drive, San Bruno, CA 94066

San Joaquin Dog Training Club, Janet Borgens, 9117 Caywood, Stockton, CA 95209

San Lorenzo Dog Training Club Inc., Martie Brown, 3490 Hackamore Drive, Hayward, CA 94541

San Mateo Dog Training Club Inc., Miss Dixie Easterby, 6077 Skyline Boulevard, Burlingame, CA 94010

Geographical List of AKC Obedience Clubs

Santa Clara Dog Training Club Inc., Beverly Cobb, 12366 Priscilla Lane, Los Altos Hills, CA 94022

Southeast Obedience Club of Lynwood Inc., Linda Scanland, 3906 Carfax Avenue, Long Beach, CA 90808

Southwest Obedience Club of Los Angeles, Ms. Vicki Margolis, 11110 Milano, Norwalk, CA 90650

Vallejo Dog Training Club, Ms. Melba Scheid, 7110 Pleasant Valley Road, Vacaville, CA 95688

Valley Hills Obedience Club, Betty Butzer, 19949 Lull Street, Canoga Park, CA 91306

Colorado
Mountain States Dog Training Club, Connie Wilson, 4392 South Vivian Way, Morrison, CO 80465

Connecticut
Nathan Hale Obedience Club, Ms. Carolyn C. Spencer, Rt. 1, Box 572, Windham Road, Brooklyn, CT 06234

Florida
Brevard County Dog Training Club, Barbara Block, P.O. Box 337, Merritt Island, FL 32952

Dog Obedience Club of Hollywood, Mrs. Sherie Janzer, 631 North 65th Avenue, Hollywood, FL 33024

Dog Training Club of St. Petersburg, Inc., Elizabeth Luttier, 9865 131st Street North, Seminole, FL 33542

Dog Training Club of Tampa, Mrs. Carol Lukes, P.O. Box 452, Durant, FL 33530

Five Flags Training of Pensacola Club, Linda Armacost, 9600 Music Lane, Pensacola, FL 32504

Imperial Polk Obedience Club of Lakeland Florida, Bonita Kaasa, 6414 Shadowbrook Lane, Lakeland, FL 33803

K-9 Obedience Club of Jacksonville, Jan Bryan, 2741 Hendricks Avenue, Jacksonville, FL 32207

Miami Obedience Club Inc., Mary Ellen Daylong, 19020 Franjo Road, Miami, FL 33157

Mary Mills, 1604 Tigertail Avenue, Miami, FL 33133

Obedience Training Club of Palm Beach County Inc., Ms. Marjorie E. Butcher, P.O. Box 6112, Lake Worth, FL 33461

Orlando Dog Training, Kathleen Morford, 1409 Barbados Avenue, Orlando, FL 32817

Sarasota Obedience Training Club, Mrs. Glendus Cosgrove, 1909 27th Avenue, West Bradenton, FL 33505

Tallahassee Dog Obedience Club, Rosilyn Harvey, Rt. 4, Box 541X9, Tallahassee, FL 32304

Upper Suncoast Dog Obedience Club, Mrs. Cecelia Lane, Drawer X, Dunedin, FL 33528

Georgia
Atlanta Obedience Club, Helen Remaley, 6034 Wandering Way, Norcross, GA 30093

Hawaii
Hilo Obedience Training Club, Rebecca Mandawe, P.O. Box 83, Hilo, HI 96720

Leeward Training Club of Hawaii Inc., Becky D. Gustafson, 94-435 Holuili Street, Mililani Town, HI 96789

Obedience Training Club of Hawaii, Twylla-Dawn Steer, 618 Paopua Loop, Kailua, HI 96734

Idaho
Upper Snake River Valley Dog Training Club, Ms. Laurie Bagley, 6809 Orlina Lane, Idaho Falls, ID

Illinois
Capitol Canine Training Club of Springfield, Mrs. Sue Price, R.R. 6, Box 90, Springfield, IL 62707

Car-Dun-Al Obedience Dog Training Club, Cindy Dennison, Rt. 1, Box 50, Elgin, IL 60120

Decatur Obedience Training Club Inc., Barb Sheay, 2306 Highland Road, Decatur, IL 62521

Forest City Dog Training Club Inc., Barbara Rasmussen, 127 Albert Avenue, Rockford, IL 61103

Fox Valley Dog Training Club, Mrs. Joseph

Geographical List of AKC Obedience Clubs

Waldeck, 2 S 607 Nelson Lake Road, Batavia, IL 60510

Glenbard All Breed Obedience Club, Judy Hirst, 240 Park Street, Winfield, IL 60190

Lincolnwood Training Club for German Shepherd Dogs, Donna Kircher, 24660 Middlefork, Barrington, IL

Lyons Township Dog Training Club, Ms. Sharon Sipla, Six Langford Court, Bolingbrook, IL 60439

North Shore Dog Training Club, Mrs. Richard Becker, 2232 Dewes, Glenview, IL 60025

Northwest Obedience Club of Suburban Chicago, Susan Gresko, 917 Stonehenge Lane, Palatine, IL 60067

Peoria Obedience Training Club, Marsha Schulze, 38 Forrest Drive, North Perkin, IL 61554

Quad Cities Dog Obedience Club Inc., Mrs. Mary Jo Ryan, 626 8th Street, Silvis, IL 61282

Rand Park Dog Training Club, Doris Mrozek, 6731 North Oliphant, Chicago, IL 60631

South Side All-Breed Dog Training Club, Mrs. Cheryl Oliver, 391 Jeffery Avenue, Calumet City, IL 60409

Westside Dog Training Club Inc., Ms. Barbara Fiene, 2176 Ash Street, Des Plaines, IL 60011

Indiana

Anderson Obedience Training Club, Ms. Shirley Spall, P.O. Box 191, Pendleton, IN 46074

Dunes Dog Training Club, Cricket Zengler, 395 Sassafras Drive, Valparaiso, IN 46383

Evansville Obedience Club, Susan Harp, 504 A Lodge Avenue, Evansville, IN 47714

Fort Wayne Obedience Training Club, Lori Losher, 5623 Centerhurst Terrace, Fort Wayne, IN 46815

Indianapolis Obedience Training Club Inc., Sue Bathauer, 1042 South Muessing Road, Indianapolis, IN 46239

Muncie Obedience Training Club, Nadenne Daugherty, RR No. 1, Box 340A, Daleville, IN 47334

Iowa

Des Moines Obedience Training Club, Elaine Wagner, 6892 Vandalia Road, RR 2, Runnells, IA 50237

Kansas

Greater Kansas City Dog Training Club, Miriam Krum, 9718 Overbrook Road, Leawood, KS 66206

Wichita Dog Training Club, Lillian Baldwin, 1710 Nottingham Court, Wichita, KS 67204

Kentucky

Greater Louisville Training Club, Nancy Gilkey, 2103 Palmer Court, New Albany, IN 47150

Louisiana

Deep South All-Breed Obedience Training Club, Lucy Marie Neeb, 1209 Field Avenue, Metairie, LA 70001

Greater New Orleans Dog Obedience Training Club Inc., Heidi Autin, 122 East 15th Street, Cut Off, LA 70345

Louisiana Capital City Obedience Club, Linda Taylor, 1423 Westchester Drive, Baton Rouge, LA 70810

Red River Obedience Training Club, Ms. Sara Correll, 832 Drexel, Shreveport, LA

Maine

Saccarappa Obedience Club, Corrie Zacharias, 31 Eureka Road, Falmouth, ME 04105

Maryland

Capital Dog Training Club of Washington, DC, Dr. Kyle H. Sibinovic, 7613 Carteret Road, Bethesda, MD 20034

Dog Owners Training Club of Maryland, Mrs. Thomas A. Knott, ToMar, 4869 Avoca Avenue, Ellicott City, MD 21043

Hyattsville Dog Training Club, Mrs. Doris Baster, 7012 Wells Parkway, Hyattsville, MD 20782

Oriole Dog Training Club, Mrs. Marsha Ellrich, 427 Croydon Road, Baltimore, MD 21212

Southern Maryland Dog Training Club of Forestville, Carla Boisseree, 1358 Constitution Avenue, NE, Washington, DC 20002

Geographical List of AKC Obedience Clubs

Massachusetts

Concord Dog Training Club, Dr. Jane Colburn, 5 Old Road, Westford, MA 01886

Holyoke Dog Obedience Training Club, Ms. Donna Blews, 85 Wisteria Street, West Springfield, MA 01089

New England Dog Training Club, Inc., Shelley Silverman, 403 Main Street, Acton, MA 01720

Shrewsbury Dog Training Club, Inc., Mrs. Elinor Rowe, 40 Edinboro Street, Marlboro, MA 01752

South Shore Dog Training Club, Inc., Edith B. Paige, 42 Marion Street, Wollaston, MA 02170

Michigan

Ann Arbor Dog Training Club, Kathy Sweet, 3172 Edgewood Drive, Ann Arbor, MI 48104

Companion Dog Training Club of Flint, Inc., Ms. Karen Bishop, G-6398 Oxbow Lane, Flint, MI 48506

Kalamazoo Dog Training Club, Joan Hines, 10162 Lloy, Portage MI 49002

Obedience Training Club of Greater Lansing, Mrs. Betty White, 10125 Sunfield Road, Sunfield, MI 48890

Southern Michigan Obedience Training Club, Mrs. Christine Kloski, 33841 Vista Way, Fraser, MI 48026

Sportsmens' Dog Training Club of Detroit, Mrs. Mira Jilbert, 2082 Butterfield, Troy, MI 48084

Minnesota

Bloomington Obedience Training Club, Ms. Clara Hovde, 9844 Blaisdell, South, Bloomington, MN 55420

Granite City Obedience Club, Ms. Joan Rathbun, Fischer's Garden Mobile Park, Sauk Rapids, MN 56379

Iron Range Dog Training Club, Marilyn J. Gjevre, P.O. Box 127, Biwabik, MN 55708

Rochester Dog Obedience Club, Julie Wallin, 310 6th Avenue N.E., Kasson, MN 55944

St. Paul Dog Training Club, Ms. Eileen Erickson, 649 23rd Avenue N.W., New Brighton, MN 55112

Twin Cities Obedience Training Club, Janice Heck, 1040-74-1/2 Avenue North, Brooklyn Park, MN 55444

Twin Ports Dog Training Club, Mrs. Becky Smith, 518 North Blackman Avenue, Duluth, MN 55811

Mississippi

Jackson Obedience Training Club, Inc., Leslie Morris, 4863 Woodmount Drive, Jackson, MS 32906

Missouri

Greater Kansas City Dog Training Club, Inc., Miriam Krum, 9718 Overbrook Road, Leawood, KS 66206

Greater St. Louis City Dog Training Club, Inc., Sue Hamm, 1921 Northfield Drive, Overland, MO 63114

Mound City Obedience Training Club, Inc., Pat Futhey, 756 Tuxedo Boulevard, St. Louis, MO 63119

Montana

Great Falls Dog Training Club, Lex Groshong, 3312 7th Avenue South, Great Falls, MT 59405

Nebraska

Greater Lincoln Obedience Club, Maurene Wurst, 308 South 5th, Milford, NE 68405

Nevada

Truckee Meadows Dog Training Club, Arlene Marshrey, P.O. Box 6029, Reno, NV 89513

Vegas Valley Dog Obedience Club, Bobbi Dreher, 8460 West Ann Road, Las Vegas, NV 89129

New Jersey

Bayshore Companion Dog Club, Inc., Mrs. JoAnn Odegaard, 34 Gayboy Court, Middletown, NJ 07747

First Dog Training Club of Northern New Jersey, Inc., Christine Lippman, 605 Montview Place, River Vale, NJ 07675

K-9 Obedience Training Club of Essex County, Miss Mary Rose Coyle, 95 Eastern Parkway, Newark, NJ 07106

Geographical List of AKC Obedience Clubs

Lower Camden County Dog Training Club, Inc., Mrs. Sandra Lyons, 356 Whitehall Rd., Williamstown, NJ 08094

Mid-Jersey Companion Dog Training Club, Inc., Ms. Sally Birgl, 9 Chestnut Street, Keyport, NJ 07035

Morris Hills Dog Training Club, Inc., Joy Cowles, P.O. Box 24, Morristown, NJ 07960

Princeton Dog Training Club, Mary Alice Hembree, 951 Brown Road, Bridgewater, NJ 08807

Town & Country Dog Training Club, Phyllis Broncrick, 133 Uncas Ave., Staten Island, NY 10309

New Mexico
Dog Obedience Club of Las Cruces, Karen Wagner, 6727 Jackrabbit, Las Cruces, NM 88047

Los Alamos Dog Obedience Club, Inc., Lynn McDowell, 2482-A 46th St., Los Alamos, NJ 87544

Sandia Dog Obedience Club, Miss Patricia Bouldin, 4626 Cairo, NE, Albuquerque, NM 87111

Santa Fe Dog Obedience Club, Susan Ptacek, Rt. 7, Box 109GP, Santa Fe, NM 87501

New York
Albany Obedience Club, Gail Jay, 2100 Fiero Avenue, Schenectady, NY 12303

Dog Obedience Training Club of Rochester, New York, Roxanne Dyer, RD 3, 5605 VanCruyning Road, Williamson, NY 14589

Nassau Dog Training Club, Mrs. Clement F. Plessner, 217 Dix Hills Road, Huntington Sta., NY 11746

Patroon Dog Training Club, Joan Butler, Ravenwood Estates, Lot 3, Johnsonville, NY 12094

Poodle Obedience Training Club of Greater New York, Ann Mandelbaum, 711 Amsterdam Avenue, New York, NY 10025

Port Chester Obedience Training Club, Mrs. Martina Ripley, 8 Barnum Road, Larchmont, NY 10538

Schenectady Dog Training Club, Ms. Winnie Martin, 168 Plank Road, Clifton Park, NY 12065

Staten Island Companion Dog Training Club, Linda Bellesi, 180 Colfax Avenue, Staten Island, NY 10306

Suffolk Obedience Training Club, Mrs. Gail Martino, 18 Surrey Lane, East Northport, NY 11731

Ulster Dog Training Club, Inc., Jeanette Goheen, 6558 Schirmer Avenue, Saugerties, NY 12477

Western Lakes Training Club of Buffalo, Elizabeth H. Frasier, 240 Woodgate Road, Tonawanda, NY 14150

North Carolina
Cape Fear Dog Training Club, Mrs. Kathie Wayman, P.O. Box 35514, Fayetteville, NC 28303

Carolina Dog Training Club, Mrs. Audie Williams, 714 Rollingwood Drive, Greensboro, NC 27410

Charlotte Dog Training Club, Tink Ormsby, Rt. 4, Box 523, Huntersville, NC 28078

Obedience Club of Asheville, Holly Guy, 17 Main Street, Asheville, NC 28803

Winston-Salem Dog Training Club, Ms. Sharon Smith, 3618 Vandalia Drive, Winston-Salem, NC 27104

Ohio
All-Breed Training Club of Akron, Miss Frances Sondles, 175 Baird Avenue, Wadsworth, OH 44281

Canton All-Breed Training Club, Kay Lowman, 6434 Circlevale St., S.E., East Canton, OH 44730

Cleveland All-Breed Training Club, Mrs. Mary Jane Mesojedec, 9332 Buena Vista Dr., Mentor, OH 44060

Columbus All-Breed Training Club, Ms. Eileen Crosby, 6333 Willowdale Ct., Columbus, OH 43229

Dayton Dog Training Club, Beverly Prisc, 2086 Bonnie Dale Drive, Bellbrook, OH 45305

Greater Toledo Obedience Training Club, Ellen

Geographical List of AKC Obedience Clubs

Leonard, 2402 Tremainsville, Toledo, OH 43613

Hamilton Dog Training Club, Inc., Tina Moore, 583 Beissinger Road, Hamilton, OH 45013

Middletown Dog Training Club, Ms. Denise Romans, 6857 Lancaster Drive, Franklin, OH

Queen City Dog Training Club, Donna Garten, 3943 Bainbridge Dr., Cincinnati, OH 45241

Tarhe All-Breed Training Club, Ms. Dorothy Davis, 115 Melcher Rd., Bucyrus, OH 44820

Youngstown All-Breed Training Club Inc., Lillian Hollen, 571 Poland Ave., Struthers, OH 44471

Oklahoma
Oklahoma City Obedience Training Club, Mrs. Wanda Morgan, 11012 N.W. 114th, Yukon, OK 73099

Tulsa Dog Training Club, Mrs. Gerald Patterson, 6647 E. 54th St., Tulsa, OK 74145

Oregon
Emerald Dog Obedience Club, Connie Alber, 39125 Deerhorn Rd., Springfield, OR 97477

Portland Dog Obedience Club, Carolyn Wray, 2043 N. Humboldt, Portland, OR 97215

Pennsylvania
Admiral Perry Obedience Training Club, Sally Bolte, RR 1, Box 176, West Springfield, PA 16443

Allentown Dog Training Club, Inc., Carole Crothers, View Drive East, Walnutport, PA 18088

Beaver Valley Training Club, Inc., Ms. Dianne McFeaters, 415 Midway Drive, Beaver, PA 15009

Berks County Dog Training Club, Inc., Mrs. Nancy Withers, 157 W. Charles Street, Wernersville, PA 19565

Dauphin Dog Training Club, Ms. Sharon D. Ehler, 10 Oake Tree Road, Hummelstown, PA 17036

Golden Triangle Obedience Training Club, Diane A'brose, 2359 Willowbrook Dr., Pittsburgh, PA 15214

Philadelphia Dog Training Club, Miss Lilian

Zentgraf, 1235 Easton Road, Warrington, PA 18976

Puerto Rico
Puerto Rico Dog Obedience Club, Cristina Bravo, 363 Lerida St., Urb. Valencia, Rio Piedras, PR 00923

Rhode Island
Obedience Training Club of Rhode Island, Mrs. John Drury, RFD 1, Box 166, Chepachet, RI 02814

South Carolina
Charleston Dog Training Club, Mickey Januszkiewicz, 904 Clifford Drive, Mt. Pleasant, SC 29464

Greater Columbia Obedience Club, Mrs. Dee Ford, Rt. 1, Box 298F, Elgin, SC 29045

Palmetto Obedience Training, Miss Josephine Prall, 332 DuPre Dr., Spartanburg, SC 29302

Tennessee
Knoxville Dog Training Club, Inc., Ms. Beth Chase, 709 Hardwick Drive, Knoxville, TN 37923

Memphis Obedience Training Club, Inc. Kay Whittington, 451 South Perkins No. 3, Memphis, TN 38117

Murfreesboro Obedience Training Club, Inc., Mrs. Cynthia Vernadakis, 1218 Delmar St., Murfreesboro, TN 37130

Nashville Dog Training Club, Nancy Gains, Rt. 9, Kari Drive, Murfreesboro, TN 37130

Obedience Club of Chattanooga, Inc., Patsy Varnell, 3316 Char Mac Ln., Chattanooga, TN 37409

Texas
Alamo Dog Obedience Club, Janice Gallager, 1710 Brogan, San Antonio, TX 78232

Capitol Dog Training Club of Austin, Susie Ayres, 12413 Limerick Ave., Austin, TX 78758

Dallas Obedience Training Club, LeLaurin Alderfer, 13839 Leinsper Green, Dallas, TX 75240

Geographical List of AKC Obedience Clubs

Ft. Worth Dog Training Club, Mrs. H.T. Stucker, 3817 Arroyo Road, Ft. Worth, TX 76109

Houston Obedience Training Dog Club, Cindy Sidell, 10838 Corona Lane, Houston, TX 77072

Obedience Training Club of Wichita Falls, Ms. Noreene Conatser, 1407 Taylor, Wichita Falls, TX 76309

Rio Grande Obedience Dog Club, John Vanderlaan, 10641 Ellington, Ft. Bliss, TX 79908

San Antonio Dog Training Club, Mary Anne Michaud, 722 W. Elsmere, San Antonio, TX 78212

South Texas Obedience Club, Beba M. Bailey, 8950 Chimney Rock 24, Houston, TX 77096

Texas Tri-City Obedience Club, Mrs. Francis V. Spencer, 7700 Davis Blvd., Ft. Worth, TX 76180

Utah
Great Salt Lake Dog Training Club, Ms. Edna Bennett, 321 Alta View Drive, Midvale, UT 84047

Vermont
Burlington Obedience Training Club, Mrs. Kathlyn Robie, RD 2, Westford Pond Road, Milton, VT 05468

Virginia
Dog Owners Training Club of Lynchburg, Frances E. White, Route 7, Box 105, Lynchburg, VA 24503

Washington
Spokane Dog Training Club, Inc., Pam Cochran, P.O. Box 53, Rt. 1, Mica, WA 99023

Washington State Obedience Training Club, Ms. Carole Hapke, 14550 Tiger Mtn. Road, SE, Isawuah, WA 98027

West Virginia
Kanawha Obedience Training Club, Nancy Aliff, 17 St. Charles Place, Charleston, WV 25314

Parkersburg Obedience Training Club, Nancy Barnhouse, 315 Montgomery Street, Marietta, OH 45750

Wisconsin
K-9 Obedience Training Club of Menomonee Falls, Sharyn Propheter, 4622 W. Stark St., Milwaukee, WI 53218

Lakeland Dog Training Club, Arlene Hildenrandt, 266 Canal Road, Rt. 2, Marshall, WI 53559

Milwaukee Dog Training Club, Inc., Diane Jahnke, 3722 So. Logan, Milwaukee, WI 53207

Index

Italic type indicates the location of color photographs.

Index

Perfect for Pet Owners!

PET OWNER'S MANUALS

Over 50 illustrations per book (20 or more color photos), 72–80 pp., paperback.

AFRICAN GRAY PARROTS (3773-1)
AMAZON PARROTS (4035-X)
BANTAMS (3687-5)
BEAGLES (3829-0)
BEEKEEPING (4089-9)
BOSTON TERRIERS (1696-3)
BOXERS (4036-8)
CANARIES (4611-0)
CATS (4442-8)
CHINCHILLAS (4037-6)
CHOW-CHOWS (3952-1)
CICHLIDS (4597-1)
COCKATIELS (4610-2)
COCKER SPANIELS (1478-2)
COCKATOOS (4159-3)
COLLIES (1875-3)
CONURES (4880-6)
DACHSHUNDS (1843-5)
DALMATIANS (4605-6)
DISCUS FISH (4669-2)
DOBERMAN PINSCHERS (2999-2)
DOGS (4822-9)
DOVES (1855-9)
DWARF RABBITS (1352-2)
ENGLISH SPRINGER SPANIELS (1778-1)
FEEDING AND SHELTERING BACKYARD
    BIRDS (4252-2)
FEEDING AND SHELTERING EUROPEAN
    BIRDS (2858-9)
FERRETS (2976-3)
GERBILS (3725-1)
GERMAN SHEPHERDS (2982-8)
GOLDEN RETRIEVERS (3793-6)
GOLDFISH (2975-5)
GOULDIAN FINCHES (4523-8)
GREAT DANES (1418-9)
GUINEA PIGS (4612-9)
GUPPIES, MOLLIES, AND PLATTIES (1497-9)
HAMSTERS (4439-8)
IRISH SETTERS (4663-3)
KEESHONDEN (1560-6)
KILLIFISH (4475-4)
LABRADOR RETRIEVERS (3792-8)
LHASA APSOS (3950-5)
LIZARDS IN THE TERRARIUM (3925-4)
LONGHAIRED CATS (2803-1)
LONG-TAILED PARAKEETS (1351-4)

LORIES AND LORIKEETS (1567-3)
LOVEBIRDS (3726-X)
MACAWS (4768-0)
MICE (2921-6)
MUTTS (4126-7)
MYNAHS (3688-3)
PARAKEETS (4437-1)
PARROTS (4823-7)
PERSIAN CATS (4405-3)
PIGEONS (4044-9)
POMERANIANS (4670-6)
PONIES (2856-2)
POODLES (2812-0)
POT BELLIES AND OTHER MINIATURE PIGS
    (1356-5)
PUGS (1824-9)
RABBITS (4440-1)
RATS (4535-1)
ROTTWEILERS (4483-5)
SCHNAUZERS (3949-1)
SCOTTISH FOLD CATS (4999-3)
SHAR-PEI (4334-2)
SHEEP (4091-0)
SHETLAND SHEEPDOGS (4264-6)
SHIH TZUS (4524-6)
SIAMESE CATS (4764-8)
SIBERIAN HUSKIES (4265-4)
SMALL DOGS (1951-2)
SNAKES (2813-9)
SPANIELS (2424-9)
TROPICAL FISH (4700-1)
TURTLES (4702-8)
WEST HIGHLAND WHITE TERRIERS (1950-4)
YORKSHIRE TERRIERS (4406-1)
ZEBRA FINCHES (3497-X)

NEW PET HANDBOOKS

Detailed, illustrated profiles (40–60 color photos), 144 pp., paperback.

NEW AQUARIUM FISH HANDBOOK (3682-4)
NEW AUSTRALIAN PARAKEET
    HANDBOOK (4739-7)
NEW BIRD HANDBOOK (4157-7)
NEW CANARY HANDBOOK (4879-2)
NEW CAT HANDBOOK (2922-4)
NEW COCKATIEL HANDBOOK (4201-8)
NEW DOG HANDBOOK (2857-0)
NEW DUCK HANDBOOK (4088-0)
NEW FINCH HANDBOOK (2859-7)
NEW GOAT HANDBOOK (4090-2)

NEW PARAKEET HANDBOOK (2985-2)
NEW PARROT HANDBOOK (3729-4)
NEW RABBIT HANDBOOK (4202-6)
NEW SALTWATER AQUARIUM
    HANDBOOK (4482-7)
NEW SOFTBILL HANDBOOK (4075-9)
NEW TERRIER HANDBOOK (3951-3)

REFERENCE BOOKS

Comprehensive, lavishly illustrated references (60–300 color photos), 136–176 pp., hardcover & paperback.

AQUARIUM FISH (1350-6)
AQUARIUM FISH BREEDING (4474-6)
AQUARIUM FISH SURVIVAL MANUAL
    (5686-8)
AQUARIUM PLANTS MANUAL (1687-4)
BEFORE YOU BUY THAT PUPPY (1750-1)
BEST PET NAME BOOK EVER, THE
    (4258-1)
CARING FOR YOUR SICK CAT (1726-9)
CAT CARE MANUAL (5765-1)
CIVILIZING YOUR PUPPY (4953-5)
COMMUNICATING WITH YOUR DOG
    (4203-4)
COMPLETE BOOK OF BUDGERIGARS
    (6059-8)
COMPLETE BOOK OF CAT CARE (4613-7)
COMPLETE BOOK OF DOG CARE (4158-5)
COMPLETE BOOK OF PARROTS (5971-9)
DOG CARE MANUAL (5764-3)
FEEDING YOUR PET BIRD (1521-3)
GOLDFISH AND ORNAMENTAL CARP
    (9286-4)
GUIDE TO A WELL BEHAVED CAT
    (1476-6)
GUIDE TO HOME PET GROOMING
    (4298-0)
HEALTHY DOG, HAPPY DOG (1842-7)
HOP TO IT: A Guide to Training Your Pet Rabbit
    (4551-3)
HORSE CARE MANUAL (1133-3)
HOW TO TALK TO YOUR CAT (1749-8)
HOW TO TEACH YOUR OLD DOG
    NEW TRICKS (4544-0)
LABYRINTH FISH (5635-3)
MACAWS (9037-3)
NONVENOMOUS SNAKES (5632-9)
WATER PLANTS IN THE AQUARIUM (3926-2)

Barron's Educational Series, Inc. • 250 Wireless Blvd., Hauppauge, NY 11788
Call toll-free: 1-800-645-3476 • In Canada: Georgetown Book Warehouse
34 Armstrong Ave., Georgetown, Ont. L7G 4R9 • Call toll-free: 1-800-247-7160
ISBN prefix: 0-8120 • Order from your favorite book or pet store

BARRON'S PET REFERENCE BOOKS

Barron's Pet Reference Books are and have long been the choice of experts and discerning pet owners. Why? Here are just a few reasons. These indispensable volumes are packed with 35 to 200 stunning full-color photos. Each provides the very latest expert information and answers questions that pet owners often wonder about.

BARRON'S PET REFERENCE BOOKS ARE:

AQUARIUM FISH (1350-6)
AQUARIUM FISH BREEDING (4474-6)
THE AQUARIUM FISH SURVIVAL MANUAL (5686-8)
BEFORE YOU BUY THAT PUPPY (1750-1)
THE BEST PET NAME BOOK EVER (4258-1)
CARING FOR YOUR SICK CAT (1726-9)
THE COMPLETE BOOK OF BUDGERIGARS (6059-8)
THE CAT CARE MANUAL (5765-1)
CIVILIZING YOUR PUPPY (4953-5)
COMMUNICATING WITH YOUR DOG (4203-4)
THE COMPLETE BOOK OF CAT CARE (4613-7)
THE COMPLETE BOOK OF DOG CARE (4158-5)
THE DOG CARE MANUAL (5764-3)

FIRST AID FOR YOUR CAT (5827-5)
FIRST AID FOR YOUR DOG (5828-3)
GOLDFISH AND ORNAMENTAL CARP (5634-5)
GUIDE TO HOME PET GROOMING (4298-0)
HEALTHY DOG, HAPPY DOG (1842-7)
HOP TO IT: A Guide to Training Your Pet Rabbit (4551-3)
THE HORSE CARE MANUAL (5795-3)
HOW TO TEACH YOUR OLD DOG NEW TRICKS (4544-0)
LABYRINTH FISH (5635-3)
THE COMPLETE BOOK OF MACAWS (6073-3)
NONVENOMOUS SNAKES (5632-9)
THE COMPLETE BOOK OF PARROTS (5971-9)
WATER PLANTS IN THE AQUARIUM (3926-2)

Barron's Educational Series, Inc., 250 Wireless Boulevard, Hauppauge, New York 11788. For faster service call toll-free: 1-800-645-3476.

In Canada: Georgetown Book Warehouse, 34 Armstrong Avenue, Georgetown, Ontario L7G 4R9. Call toll-free: 1-800-247-7160.

Books can be purchased at your bookstore or directly from Barron's. Enclose check or money order for total amount plus sales tax where applicable and 10% for postage (minimum charge $3.75. Can. $4.00). All major credit cards are accepted. Prices subject to change without notice. ISBN Prefix: 0-8120